BRAIN GAMES™

Lower Your Brain Age in Minutes a Day

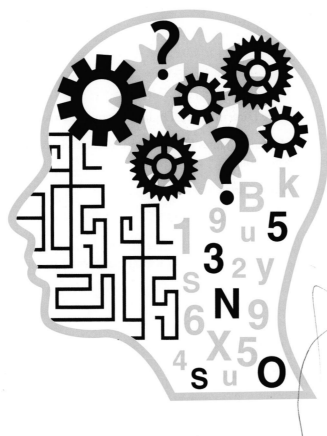

Publications International, Ltd.

Introduction by: Patti Celori Said, Executive Director, New England Cognitive Center

Puzzlers: Kelly Clark, Jeanette Dall, Mark Danna, James Harvey Estes, Patrick Merrell, Ellen Pill, Paul Seaburn, Fraser Simpson, Linda Washington

Illustrators: Bryan Babiarz, Connie Formby, Cristina Martin

Louis Weber, CEO
Publications International, Ltd.
7373 North Cicero Avenue
Lincolnwood, Illinois 60712

Permission is never granted for commercial purposes.

ISBN-13: 978-1-4127-1392-4
ISBN-10: 1-4127-1392-7

Manufactured in China.

8 7 6 5 4 3 2 1

CONTENTS

Brain Fitness

Healthy longevity—it's something we all want. We want to live long, full lives and maintain our independence for as long as possible. To do this, we must keep our minds and bodies in good working order. Most people know that one of the keys to living a long, healthy life is physical fitness, and we understand the importance of remaining active. Walking, swimming, and other exercises, along with following a healthy diet, are excellent ways of keeping our bodies in shape as time passes.

Another important key to healthy longevity is emotional fitness. We need to be with family and friends, to have good support networks, and to avoid stress and depression as much as possible. Volunteering, participating in group activities, and keeping in touch with friends and family are a few ways to help stay emotionally fit. Fun and laughter keep the blues away, and they help us maintain our emotional fitness.

The third key to healthy longevity is cognitive fitness—keeping our brains stimulated and active. Not only is the brain the "control center" of the body, but it is the storehouse of our memories. The brain determines our behaviors—it literally makes us who we are. Our brains are as unique as our fingerprints and our faces. Thanks in part to advances in technology, researchers have been able to develop a better understanding of how the brain works. In fact, we have learned more about the workings of the human brain in the last decade than in all of history. Because we have a better understanding of the way the brain works, we now know how to better maintain it.

So, how can you stay cognitively fit? The first thing to do is to rethink your position. Start by replacing in your mind the old adage "You can't teach an old dog new tricks" with a new slogan: "Use it or lose it!" The brain loves to learn and to experience new things—it is stimulated by novelty, and it thrives on challenge. If something is routine or too easy, our brains are not challenged, and we are essentially operating on autopilot, which does not require a lot of thought and does little to maintain cognitive fitness. Therefore, we need to find ways to exercise our brains, keeping them sharp, strong, and fit. Learning and trying new things stimulates the brain. Whether you attempt to learn a new language, a new knitting technique, or how to square dance, you are giving your brain a workout. And sometimes something old can be new again—like picking up that violin or sitting down at the piano, even if it has been decades since you played your last note. The more you have to think and remember, the more you are exercising your brain. If something is too easy, your brain is not working hard. On the other hand, if something is too difficult, you can become frustrated and give up, so that the brain gets little or no workout.

We all know that puzzles are fun to solve, but are they good for our brains? Most experts agree that they are. Many gerontologists and physicians recommend working puzzles as one way of staying mentally active. Puzzles require attention and concentration, help stimulate memory, and require the use of problem-solving skills, all of which are important cognitive functions. We can think of puzzles as mini workouts for our brains, and if this is the case, we should try to maximize the benefit that we get from these mental workouts. How do we do this? Let's look at a few tips that will help you use puzzles to get the best brain workout.

First things first—spend a minute or two selecting the type of puzzle and the level of difficulty. There are many different types of puzzles, and most people just choose a puzzle that they like to do and one that they can probably finish rather easily. This is fine if you are using the puzzles for entertainment. However, if you want to maximize your brain workout, you need to use a little more care in the selection process. Remember that the brain loves novelty, so try not to work the same kind of puzzle day after day. Vary the types of puzzles that you work. Different types of puzzles stimulate different parts of the brain,

and you want to work as many of these parts as possible. To help in your selection, we've labeled each puzzle with the cognitive function it exercises. Consider doing a few different types of puzzles each day. If you only work crossword puzzles, for example, you may get very good at solving this type of puzzle, but you are limiting the scope of your workout. It's an excellent idea to spend about an hour a day working a variety of puzzles. For example, work a puzzle that uses words, one that uses numbers, and then a logic problem or a maze. Choose puzzles that make you think. Feel the cogs spinning as you search for answers. Like physical fitness, cognitive fitness can be the result of workouts that are consistent and appropriately challenging.

Don't forget that puzzles are portable. They can travel with you to the park, the beach, or the dentist's office. Why not turn your downtime into brain-boosting time? It can also be enjoyable working puzzles with other people. This is a great way to keep emotionally fit. So, next time you want to give yourself a physical, emotional, and cognitive workout, grab that puzzle book, walk over to a friend's house, and get to work. Oh, and don't forget—have fun!

Patti Celori Said
Executive Director
New England Cognitive Center

Here are a variety of puzzles designed to give your brain a healthy warm-up.

The House

SPATIAL VISUALIZATION **LANGUAGE**

Every word listed is contained within this group of letters. The words can be found horizontally, vertically, or diagonally. They may read either backward or forward.

ATTIC	BEDROOM	CHIMNEY	DOMICILE	LIVING ROOM
BALCONY	BRICK	CLOSET	DOOR	LOCK
BASEMENT	CARPET	CUP	DRAPES	MANTELPIECE
BATHROOM	CEILING	DEN	DRESSER	MAT
BED	CELLAR	DINING ROOM	DRIVEWAY	MIRROR
		DISH	FLOOR	NEST
		DOMESTICITY	FOUNDATION	NURSERY
			FURNITURE	PANE
			GARAGE	PICTURE
			GARDEN	PORCH
			HALL	ROOF
			HEARTH	RUG
			HOME	SHOWER
			KEY	SIDING
			KITCHEN	SINK
			LAMP	SLATE
				SOFA
				STAIRCASE
				STOOP
				STOVE
				TABLE
				TERRACE
				TILE
				VASE
				VERANDA
				WALL
				WINDOW
				WOOD
				YARD

```
                  T M
                K R I A
            H K C O L N              P
          H A L L I O E T        E O P
          Y A W E V I R D N E    L R U
        C A R P E T D N B E L L  I C C
      C T E R R A C E R T M Y T P C H H
      I E N E D          E E E P O I O N
      T D I N L        K S L A M M E B E
      T O U L F        O A S N E O E C O D
      A O A W I O G S L M B E E E D E B E L R T B M R
      F W E I S N O C H O Y N U R S E R Y E T A L S A W
      U D I N I N G R O O M E O E G A R A G T M G E L N
      R N M D A      R W O H      C U H        S L E
      N E I O D      G M E T      R R S        A E H
      I S R W N      N F L R      O I I        V C C
      T T R P A      I L B A L C O N Y E A F O S T T
      U O O M R      V O A E H M K O E R U T C I P I
      R O R A E      I O T H M D R A P E S H S I D K
      E P E L V      L R D R A Y T I C I T S E M O D
```

Answers on page 86.

Anagrammed to Homonyms

An anagram is a word made up of the rearranged letters of another word (as in *made* and *dame*). Homonyms are two words that have the same sound but different spellings (as in *here* and *hear*). Anagram each pair of words below to form a pair of homonyms.

EARL – – – LEER

KEEL – – – LAKE

LEAN – – – NAIL

MATE – – – TEEM

OARS – – – ROSE

Seven Slices

SPATIAL VISUALIZATION   PROBLEM SOLVING

Divide the large circle with three straight lines so that there is only one small circle in each segment.

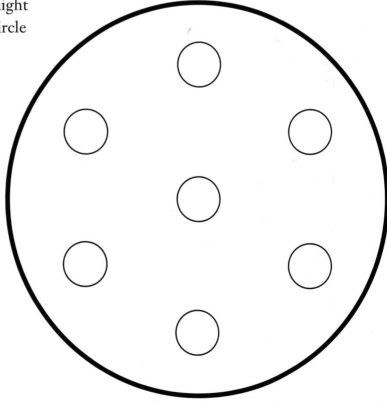

Answers on page 86.

Patriotic Songs

ACROSS

1. Emotional shock
5. Stare at the stars
9. Mr. T's squad, with "The"
14. Kind of rug
15. Most populous continent
16. Creator of Winnie the Pooh
17. 1995 hit song by TLC
20. Enjoys a bath
21. Two times five
22. Came closer to
26. Fully gratify a desire
30. Holiday song crooned by Crosby
34. "The Man Who Mistook His
    Wife for ___ ___"
35. Boxer Spinks who beat Ali
36. Skins an apple
37. Sprees
39. Last name of Stallone's Rocky
40. An inert gas
41. Rocky for Stallone
44. A lot of
45. Footwear in an Elvis Presley song
48. Nile snakes
49. Must
50. One ___ ___ time
51. Sheriff's star
56. What the answers to 17-, 30-,
    and 45-Across contain
63. Harvests
64. Ark builder
65. Sigh word
66. With 32-Down, newswoman Linda
    Ellerbee's tag line
67. Japanese wrestling
68. Title fish in a 2003 animated movie

DOWN

1. Containers
2. Three-layer cookie
3. She dallied with a swan
4. Speak
5. Practical joke
6. ___ Wednesday
7. Pimple
8. Defunct airline
9. Prayer ending
10. First X or O in a 3-in-a-row game
11. Yale student
12. Santa ___ winds
13. Actor/director Gibson
18. Ain't right?
19. Prefix for cure or cab
23. Shocking fish
24. Top card
25. Greek letter before sigma
26. Patron saint of sailors
27. One-celled organisms
28. Eagle's claws
29. Test that's not true/false
30. Spins
31. End a phone call
32. See 66-Across
33. Health resort
34. Addis ___ (capital of Ethiopia)
38. Naval rank: Abbr.
39. Tops
41. Once again gains money or trust

42. Poem of praise
43. Was ahead
46. "For ___ us a child is born…"
47. Traveling tramp
50. In addition
52. Actor Alda
53. Loser to Clinton
54. Unit of mass
55. Old gas brand
56. "… ___ ___ mouse?"
57. Famed KC QB Dawson
58. Mom's spouse
59. In-car location finder
60. With 56-Down, "Are ___ a man…"
61. America's uncle
62. Korean-American comic Margaret

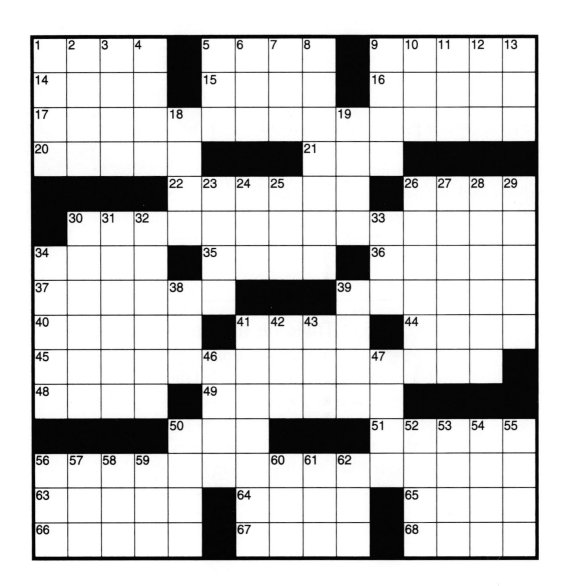

Answers on page 86.

Don't Forget to Count the Donuts

PROBLEM SOLVING

MEMORY   LANGUAGE

On Police Officer Appreciation Day at the Bear Clause Donut Shop and Law Firm, all local officers who came in uniform got to eat as many donuts as they wanted. Thirty men and women in blue showed up and chowed down. When the cloud of powdered sugar finally settled and the satisfied officers left, the clerk realized she had forgotten to write down how many donuts each officer had eaten. The legal branch of the Bear Clause Donut Shop and Law Firm informed her that by some obscure law, she must report the total number of officers who ate 6, 7, 8, or 9 donuts so they can be written off as a charitable donation (or in this case, a "donution"). All the poor clerk can remember is that 10 of the officers ate fewer than 6 donuts, 8 ate more than 7 donuts, 5 ate more than 8 donuts, and one ate more than 9 donuts. Can you help the clerk stay out of trouble with her bosses and figure out how many officers ate 6, 7, 8, or 9 donuts?

Trivia on the Brain

Fevers are controlled by the part of the brain called the hypothalamus. The highest body temperature ever recorded was 115 degrees Fahrenheit. Temperatures greater than 109 degrees can be fatal.

Answers on page 86.

All Twenty-Six

Use all 26 letters of the alphabet once and only once to complete this mini-crossword puzzle.

ACROSS

2. Perpendicular measurement
5. Military organization: abbr.
8. Alcoholic beverages
9. Sports center, for short

DOWN

1. Second month: abbr.
3. Entertaining machine: abbr.
4. Doves' opponents
6. Bring bad luck
7. Comfy

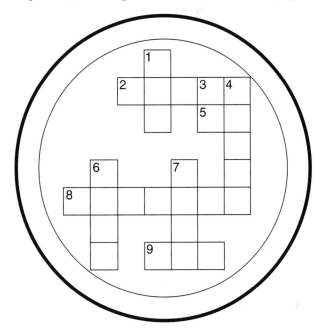

Assemblage of As

VISUAL DISCRIMINATION   PERCEPTION

Within this picture is an assemblage of things beginning with the letter "A." We count 16. How many can you find?

Answers on page 86.

Honeycomb

There are 16 letters in the honeycomb below that are surrounded by different letters (no letters are repeated). Can you find them all?

Three-Letter Anagrams

Fill in the blanks in each sentence below with words that are anagrams (rearrangements of the same letters) of one another.

1. My _____ can _____ numbers better than yours.

2. _____ is my favorite month to eat a _____.

3. When Dad found out he'd eaten a _____ fish, our home was a battle site for the third world _____.

4. The _____ of a lion's day is spent in the _____.

5. Lao-Tse never _____ until the _____ was poured.

Answers on page 86.

It's Tricky! (Part I)

Jocko the Magnificent is a great magician, but he has a problem: He doesn't always remember which props he uses in his magic act. See if you can help. First, study this picture for two minutes. Then turn the page for a quiz on what you've seen.

It's Tricky! (Part II)

(DON'T READ THIS PUZZLE UNTIL YOU HAVE READ THE PREVIOUS PAGE.)

Three of the props pictured here belong to another magician and did NOT appear on the preceding page. From memory, can you figure out which ones they are?

Answers on page 86.

The "T" Sound

Every word listed below is contained within this group of letters. Words can be found horizontally, vertically, or diagonally. They may read either backward or forward. Leftover letters tell what "T is for" according to an old song.

CANTEEN

COUNTY

ESTEEM

PRETTY

STEAM

STEEP

STEER

TEACHER

TEAK

TEASE

TEENY-BOPPER

TEETER-TOTTER

TEETH

T-SQUARE

```
M  E  E  T  S  E  T  I  C  A  N  T  E  E  N
S  F  O  T  S  Q  U  A  R  E  T  E  A  S  E
R  T  H  R  E  T  T  O  T  R  E  T  E  E  T
E  T  E  A  R  A  S  S  K  H  S  E  S  H  E
         D  C  A  T  T
         S  E  H  E  T
         T  O  A  E  S
         E  M  A  N  R
         E  V  P  Y  H
         P  Y  R  B  T
         R  T  E  O  E
         E  N  T  P  E
         E  U  T  P  T
         T  O  Y  E  E
         S  C  M  R  E
```

Trivia on the Brain

There are approximately 100 billion neurons in the human brain, which allows information to travel at speeds up to 268 miles per hour.

Answers on page 86.

Lip Service

ACROSS

1. "Yikes"
5. Lumberyard tools
9. "Hungarian Rhapsodies" composer Franz
14. Employee's move, for short
15. "___ Silver! Away!"
16. "...an old woman who lived in ___ ___"
17. Comfy footwear
20. Popular swimwear brand
21. Leaves the dock
22. One of Alcott's "Little Women"
24. Agnus ___ (Lamb of God)
25. Nine-digit ID org.
26. Scrooge's expletive
29. Practice boxing
31. Session: abbr.
33. Jai ___
35. Swift, compact horse
37. Exhorts
41. Shears for a hair pro
44. Foe
45. Beer foam
46. Basic seasoning
47. Harden
49. Miffed state
51. Domicile: abbr.
52. Spot of land in the Seine
55. Opening
57. Mrs. David Copperfield
59. Tinny-sounding
62. "Give a ring sometime!"
66. Griddle utensils
68. Soft Dutch cheeses
69. Repetitive learning process
70. Does a gardening chore
71. Zaps with a stun gun
72. Lith. and Ukr., formerly
73. Assistant

DOWN

1. Eyes, poetically
2. Dickens's Uriah
3. Like many a New England "shoppe"
4. Mount in Exodus
5. Have a good day on the links
6. Prepare to fire
7. "Swiss Family Robinson" author Johann
8. Did a cobbler's job
9. Enjoys thoroughly, as praise, slangily
10. AOL and others
11. Mets' stadium's dedicatee et al.
12. Geisha's footwear
13. Inventor and electrical engineer Nikolai
18. Praise-filled poems
19. News bit
23. Severe
26. Like a ___ in the woods
27. Actor Alda
28. Loser to the tortoise
30. Track meet events
32. Orgs.
34. Some PCs
36. Not at all spicy
38. Equipment
39. ___ Stanley Gardner
40. Retired sound-breakers
42. Monocle

43. Extreme follies
48. Use a phone
50. Ensnare
52. Egg on
53. "You can ___ ___ horse to water..."
54. Old lab burners
56. Marina sights

58. First Greek letter
60. Topmost
61. Corp. money chiefs
63. First of 13 popes
64. Classic TV's talking horse
65. Caesar's existence
67. Env. content, maybe

Answers on page 87.

Rectangle Census

How many rectangles of all sizes are formed by the lines in this diagram? Although there are fewer than 15 rectangles, many people count incorrectly when they try this puzzle. How will you do?

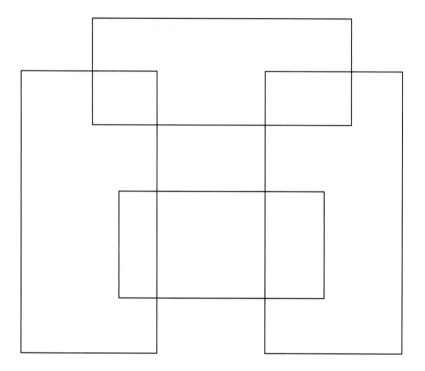

Hint: Label each separate region of the diagram with a letter and make a list of letter combinations that form rectangles.

Hello, My Name Is Wrong

The meeting was about to start, the two guest speakers had not yet arrived, and Sally, the meeting planner, had a dilemma. She had filled out name tags for everyone but the speakers because she couldn't remember their names. All she knew was that their first names were Morey and Les, and their last names were Thyme and Munny. She decided to fill out three tags with the names Morey Thyme, Morey Munny, and Les Munny and hope two of them were right. The guest speakers finally showed up and laughed when they saw the name tags. They promised not to tell Sally's boss that two of the name tags were wrong if she could tell them their real names. Sally needed the money from this job so she took her time and figured it out. What were the guests' names?

Answers on page 87.

Maze:
Soupy Sailfish

START

FINISH

Answers on page 87.

Continuous
Line Bet

Draw four straight lines to bisect these circles. Do not lift your pencil from the page. Do not double back.

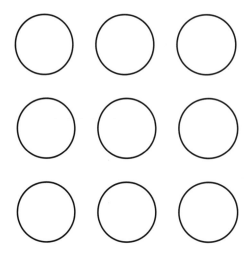

Sum-thing
to Puzzle Over

Fill in the blank spaces with numbers 1 through 9. The numbers in each row must add up to the sums in the right-hand column. The numbers in each column must add up to the sums on the bottom line. The numbers in each diagonal must add up to 15.

			15
	2		6
4		6	15
7	8		24
12	15	18	15

Answers on page 87.

Game On!

PROBLEM SOLVING   MEMORY   LANGUAGE

Fill each square of the grid with one of the four letters of the word GAME so that each row, each column, and *both diagonals* contain all four letters. We've inserted four letters to get you started.

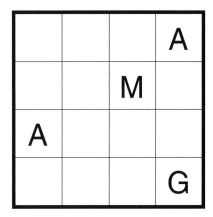

Word Ladders

MEMORY   RECALL   FLEXIBILITY

Change just one letter on each line to go from the top word to the bottom word. Do not change the order of the letters.

1. SNAP

_____

_____

_____

   SHOT

2. MILK

_____

_____

   PAIL

3. LAKE

_____

_____

_____

   MEAD

4. SAIL

_____

_____

   BOAT

5. ROSE

_____

_____

_____

   BUDS

Answers on page 87.

21

STRETCH YOUR BRAIN

In this section, the puzzles are harder. We've added grid mazes, number crosswords, and some new visual puzzles to boost the challenge.

Number Diamond

SPATIAL VISUALIZATION

COMPUTATION

Arrange the numbers 1 through 9 in the circles below so that any three circles on a straight line total 15. Use each number only once.

Hint: The sum of the two outside numbers on each line will be the same.

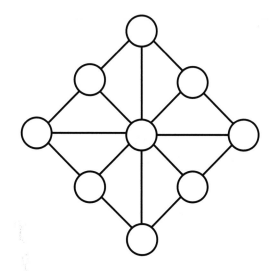

Bottom of the Dice

SPATIAL VISUALIZATION

COMPUTATION

You can't see the bottoms of the dice below, but can you determine the total number of dots on them anyway?

Hint: Opposite sides of standard dice always add up to the same number.

Answers on page 87.

Honeycomb Crossword

Answer each definition with a six-letter word. Write the words in a clockwise direction around the numerals in the grid. Words overlap each other and may start in any of the spaces around the numerals. We've positioned some letters to get you started.

1. Incorporate
2. Envelop
3. Blundered
4. Servile follower
5. Luxuriate
6. Courting
7. Climbed
8. Seized with fingernails
9. Spice

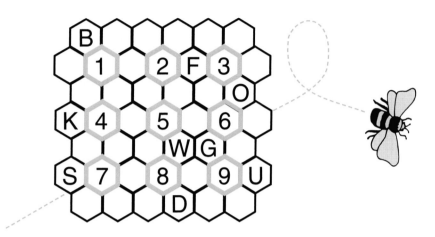

More Word Ladders

Change just one letter on each line to go from the top word to the bottom word. Each line will contain a new word. Do not change the order of the letters.

1. FOOT

_____

_____

_____

BALL

2. SNOW

_____

_____

_____

FORT

3. SIDE

_____

_____

WALK

4. LEFT

_____

_____

HAND

Answers on pages 87–88.

Four-Letter Anagrams

Fill in the blanks in each sentence below with words that are anagrams (rearrangements of the same letters) of one another.

1. The magician always waves his _____ at the crack of _____.

2. Junior played a _____ in setting the mouse _____.

3. This blindfold doesn't _____ you from sneaking a _____.

4. This barbeque _____ is so big it requires not one, but two _____.

5. A _____ water skier stays in the _____ of the boat.

6. _____-flying _____ go hungry.

7. I've heard the _____ delivery in _____, Peru, is unreliable.

8. The brewery's four best _____ are rarely on _____.

9. If your _____ of soup is too hot it is a good idea to _____ on it.

10. The _____ of dinner cooking came through the kitchen _____.

11. If you want a slice of _____ in your drink, you'll have to walk a _____ to the nearest store.

12. I don't _____ who wins the horse _____.

13. Cain's brother _____ was a very _____ farmer.

14. A great river like the _____ in Egypt rarely flows in a straight _____.

15. The student went to climb the _____ with a few of his _____ from school.

Trivia on the Brain

The average adult human brain weighs about 3 pounds and makes up about 2% of the total body weight. The heaviest brain ever recorded weighed 5 pounds, 1.1 ounces.

Answers on page 88.

Barbershop Duet

Something has gone drastically wrong in this barbershop. We count 7 wrong things. Can you find them all?

Number Gridlock

PROBLEM SOLVING

COMPUTATION

Fill each square of the grid with a number between 1 and 9 so that the product of the digits in each row or column is equal to the number that appears to the right of that row or at the bottom of that column. Important: the number 1 can only be used once in any row or column; other numbers can be repeated. Some numbers may not be used at all.

Hint: Some of the squares contain 5s and 7s. Identify these first.

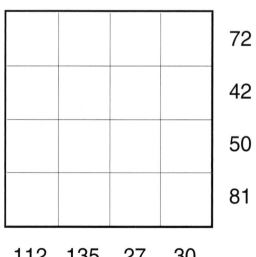

Answers on page 88.

Jumble of Js

Within this picture is a jumble of things beginning with the letter J. We count 9 things. Can you find them all?

It's Easier at the Dollar Store

Shopping Sally lived in an upscale neighborhood where there were no stores where everything cost a dollar. However, there was a unique high-class emporium called Jefferson & Lincoln, which only allowed shoppers to purchase items using two-dollar bills (with Jefferson's picture on the front) and five-dollar bills (featuring a picture of Lincoln). Sally stopped at the bank on the way to the store and picked up 10 twos and 10 fives. That meant she could buy items that cost up to $70. However, there were four items Sally couldn't buy. If all prices are in dollars only (no cents), how much did they cost?

Answers on page 88.

Around the World in 20 Minutes

Every word listed below is contained within this group of letters. The words can be found horizontally, vertically, or diagonally. They may read backward or forward.

ANGOLA

AUSTRIA

BRAZIL

CANADA

CHINA

DENMARK

FINLAND

FRANCE

GERMANY

GREAT BRITAIN

GREECE

ICELAND

IRAN

IRELAND

ISRAEL

ITALY

JAPAN

ROMANIA

SPAIN

SWEDEN

TURKEY

```
                    A   D   P   N   S
                N   N   E   G   A   C   Y
            G   A   P   A   R   R   B   A   T
        O   L   B   A   N   E   I   E   R   N   L
    L   N   D   E   N   M   A   R   K   E   E   A   R
A   I   N   A   M   O   R   T   A   F   A   C   H   D   O
F   Z   I   M   B   E   U   B   U   R   C   H   E   R   A
G   A   T   A   M   R   O   R   S   A   L   I   S   D   O
I   R   A   J   K   O   M   I   T   N   A   N   N   Y   I
E   B   L   E   A   S   Y   T   R   C   H   A   N   R   S
    J   Y   G   O   P   T   A   I   E   L   A   E   W
        Z   B   P   Q   A   I   A   E   M   L   E
            S   P   A   I   N   C   R   A   D
                T   O   V   I   E   N   E
                    M   A   G   D   N
```

Answers on page 88.

Crossing Caution

ACROSS

1. Bovine baby
5. Shankar of sitar
9. Synagogue official
14. Cain's brother
15. Seuss's "If __ __ the Zoo"
16. Kept in the dark
17. Fish in a melt
18. Unsteady gait
19. City near Florence
20. Breaking news order
23. Protrudes
24. Vine-covered
25. Sporty Chevy
28. Sneaker brand
29. New Deal prog.
32. Big name in gas
33. Furnace output
34. Restaurateur Toots
35. "You're one to spout off!"
38. Lodging providers
39. Skin moisturizer
40. Perform better than
41. NFL 3-pointers
42. Type of school
43. Annoy forcefully
44. Caribbean republic
46. Challenging chore
47. "Think it over"
52. Titanic-seeker's tool
53. Cry of frustration
54. Boat follower
55. Office worker
56. Cold war defense assn.
57. Former blade brand
58. Soda insert
59. Kind of jacket
60. Wine list datum

DOWN

1. Rodent exterminators
2. Share a border
3. Jay of TV
4. Pancakes
5. "Sure thing!"
6. Ovine sign
7. Theda Bara role
8. Behind closed doors
9. Putin's land
10. Liqueur flavoring
11. Use all the resources of
12. Waste containers
13. "Give ___ ___ rest"
21. Novelist Scott
22. Madonna musical
25. Ariz. neighbor
26. In the midst of
27. White lightning maker
28. Noted fabulist
30. Polliwogs' places
31. Job-specific vocabulary
33. Golfer's dream
34. Leave stealthily
36. Author Bret
37. At large
42. NASCAR service area
43. Strand on an island
45. Yoga posture

46. Jay Silverheels role

47. Senator Trent

48. What this isn't

49. Glut

50. Gumbo vegetable

51. Get closer to

52. Draft letters

Trivia on the Brain
A brain can go without blood flow for 8–10 seconds before consciousness is lost.

Answers on page 88.

Word of Mouth

Fill each square with one of the five letters of the word MOUTH so that each row, each column, and both diagonals contain all five letters exactly once. We've inserted six letters to get you started.

T		H		M
	T			
			M	
U				

What's Flipped in Vegas, Stays in Vegas

Vivian loved Las Vegas. After seeing all the hottest shows, eating at all the hottest buffets, and walking down all the hottest sidewalks, Vivian was ready to try and get hot at gambling. Unfortunately, the only game she knew was flipping coins. Luckily, she found Caesar's Shack, a tiny casino that catered to coin flippers. The croupier—or in this case, flipier—invited her to play the house game. He would let her flip a coin 20 times. Each time the coin landed on heads, he would pay her $2. Each time the coin landed on tails, she had to pay him $3. Vivian was on edge but decided to give it a try. She flipped the coin 20 times and left Caesar's Shack with the same amount of money she came in with. How many times did the coin come up heads?

> ## ⚙⚙ Trivia on the Brain
> Albert Einstein's brain weighed about 2 pounds, 11.4 ounces—far below the average brain weight of 3 pounds.

Answers on page 88.

Match-Up Twins

The 10 hexagons below may look identical at first glance, but they're not. They can actually be divided into 5 pairs of identical designs. Can you match them up?

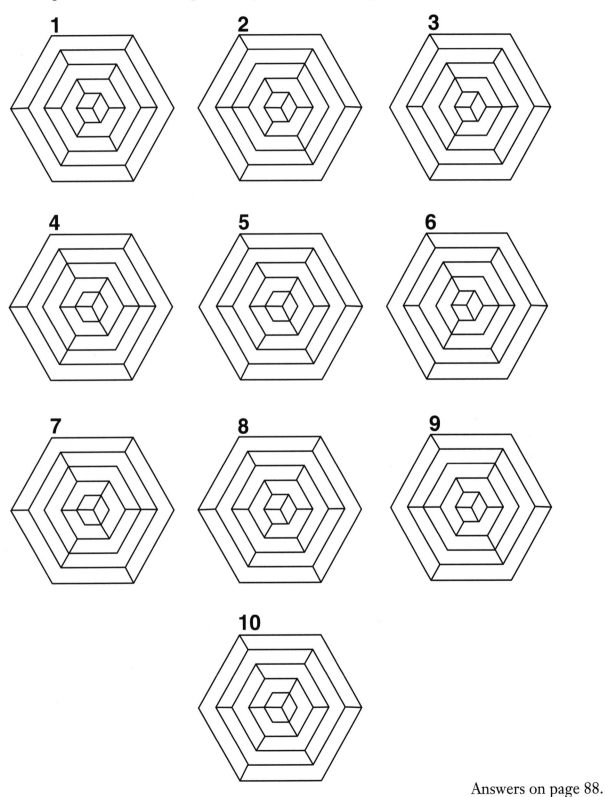

Answers on page 88.

Add It Up

Fill in the blank spaces with numbers between 1 and 9. The numbers in each row must add up to the sums in the right-hand column. The numbers in each column must add up to the sums on the bottom line. The numbers in each diagonal must add up to the sums in the upper and lower right corners.

						25
	4	6		2	4	26
1			7	9	1	26
4	6	8		4		30
9		5	3		9	34
2	4		8	1		24
	3	5	7		1	26
19	27	35	35	26	24	18

Age-Old Question

Next year I will be 21 but just 2 days ago I was 18. Hard to believe? There is only one day of the year—my birthday—that could make my opening statement true. What day is my birthday, and on what day did I make this statement?

Answers on page 88.

Retro
Rocket Maze

Answers on page 89.

Take a Number

Fill in this crossword with numbers instead of letters. Use the clues to determine which of the numbers 1 through 9 belongs in each square. No zeros are used.

ACROSS

1. Consecutive digits, ascending
4. A number of the form ABAB
6. A palindrome
8. Consecutive digits, ascending

DOWN

1. A square
2. A palindrome
3. Consecutive digits, ascending
5. Its third digit is the sum of its first two digits
7. Both of its digits are odd

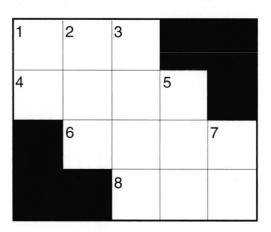

Name Search

SPATIAL VISUALIZATION PROBLEM SOLVING LANGUAGE

Two friends had a contest to see who could hide their name more times in this grid. One of them won by only one! Reading their three-letter names forward, backward, up, down, and diagonally, can you figure out the winner?

Each of them has also hidden the same three-letter spherical object in the grid once. Can you find both places where it appears?

Answers on page 89.

Circle Takes the Square

All you have to do to solve this puzzle is move in a single, unbroken path from the circle in the upper left corner to the circle in the lower right. Your path must alternate between circles and squares, and you can only move horizontally and vertically (not diagonally). There's only one way to do it.

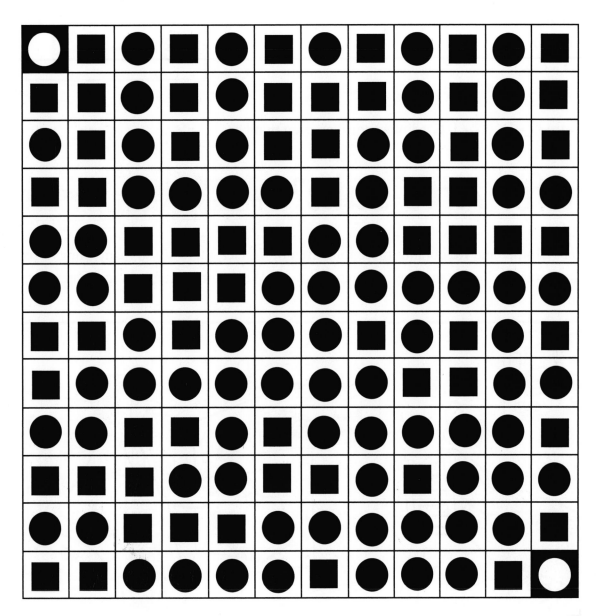

Answers on page 89.

Letters to Numbers

Each letter represents a number from 1 through 9.
Use the clues to help you put the numbers in their
places within the grid.

Clues:
1. $G \times G = F + H$
2. $B \times G \times J = A$
3. $B \times D = D$
4. $D + D = G + J$
5. $E + H = B + C + F$

A	B	C
D	E	F
G	H	J

Hint: Since $D + D = G + J$, $G + J$ must equal an even number.

Art for Art's Sake?

Whistler's Mother and Rembrandt these folks are not! In fact, there are so many things wrong
with this picture we're not sure we can even call it art. We count 9 wrong things. Can you find
them all?

Answers on page 89.

Can You Conjugate a Beatle?

While on a round-the-world solo sailing trip, Maggie Ellen thought she had packed everything she needed. When an unexpected tropical storm blew her tiny boat aground on the small Pacific island of Uma-Uma, she realized she forgot to bring the one thing that would help her there: an Uma-Uma-to-English translation guide. The only thing she could remember was that the Uma-Uma language was made up entirely of the first names of famous rock-and-roll stars. By listening carefully to the Uma-Umas speak while pointing to different things, she figured out that "John Paul George" meant large apple tree, "George Ringo" meant small tree, and "Paul Chubby" meant large coconut. What name did Maggie Ellen have to say to tell the Uma-Umas she wanted an apple?

Number Challenge

Fill in this crossword with numbers instead of letters. Use the clues to determine which of the numbers 1 through 9 belongs in each square. No zeros are used.

ACROSS

1. A multiple of 7
3. A prime number
5. Consecutive digits, ascending
7. 700 more than 10-across
8. Five different odd numbers, out of order
10. 10 more than 11-across
11. A multiple of 5

DOWN

1. A multiple of 11
2. Five different odd numbers, out of order
3. A palindrome that is 8-across minus 2-down
4. The square of an even square
6. The first and last digits add up to the middle digit
8. A multiple of 11
9. A multiple of 3

Answers on page 89.

37

MEET THE CHALLENGE

For this level, we've added sequencing exercises, as well as puzzles that test your ability to rotate shapes in space. The other puzzles are also more challenging, to give your brain an extra workout.

To the Letter   PROBLEM SOLVING   COMPUTATION

Each letter represents a number between 1 and 9. No zeros are used. Can you determine the set of letter values that will make all of the equations work?

Hint: Start by listing all of the combinations of three different digits that add up to 9.

$$A + B + C = 9$$
$$B + D + E = 11$$
$$A + B + B = 13$$
$$E + E + F = 15$$

Misleading Sequence   PROBLEM SOLVING   ANALYSIS

Circle the two numbers in the progression below, which when added together equal 18.

$$1\ 2\ 3\ 4\ 5\ 6\ 7\ 8\ 9$$

Next Color?   PROBLEM SOLVING   ANALYSIS

What is the next color in this familiar progression of colors?

Yellow, blue, red, purple, orange, green, plum, _____

Answers on page 89.

Diagonal Switch

Can you find a single, unbroken path from the circle in the upper left corner to the circle in the lower right? If you move horizontally or vertically, you must move only to the same shape (for example, from a square to a square). You must change shapes when you move diagonally. There's only one way to do it.

Trivia on the Brain
The first lobotomy in the United States was performed by Walter Freeman in 1936.

Answers on page 89.

Awfully Nice

ACROSS

1. Korea's continent
5. Napoleon's isle of exile
9. Wedding party transports
14. Shellac ingredients
15. Refrigerate
16. "___ ___ a Parade"
17. Fill-in for a talk show, e.g.
19. Chimney channels
20. Dress, as a judge
21. "Ditto"
23. Imp
24. Got up
25. Decompose
27. London cathedral
31. Mexican money
35. Forty winks
37. Bisects
38. Strong glue
40. Teacher's favorite
42. Explosive experiment, for short
43. Colored anew
45. Hit with a stun gun
47. Panamas and boaters
48. Joins forces (with)
50. Practical joke
52. "___ ___ mio!"
54. Search parties, in the Old West
59. Retaliation
62. Geritol target
63. Mistake
64. "Heavens!"
66. Skirt style
67. Until
68. "I cannot tell ___ ___"
69. Singer/actress Della
70. Fair hiring org.
71. Big wigs in biz

DOWN

1. Horatio of inspirational books
2. Spa spot
3. Bakery employees
4. Org.
5. Level of authority
6. Toilet, in London
7. "Blame it on the ___ Nova"
8. Sanctuary centerpieces
9. Threescore and ten, maybe
10. Sickness
11. Pout
12. Finished
13. Ousted Zaire ruler Mobuto ___ Seko
18. Way up the ski slope
22. Wool-eating insect
26. Faucet
28. Middle layer of the eye
29. "___ we forget"
30. Grounded sound breakers: Abbr.
31. Saucy, as a young lass
32. Pointless fencing sword
33. Fountain treat
34. What 17 Across, 64 Across, 10 Down, and this puzzle's title are
36. Dispenser candy
39. "You betcha!"
41. "You're it!" chasing game

44. Performing twosomes
46. One time Haitian dictator, informally
49. One of ten in Exodus
51. Bell hit with a hammer
53. Wed on the run
55. Glacial ridge

56. Photographer's request
57. Old MacDonald's refrain
58. Bank vaults
59. Back side
60. ___ Stanley Gardner
61. ___-dieu (prayer bench)
65. Oklahoma Native American

Answers on page 90.

Anagrammatically Correct

Fill in the blanks in each sentence below with four-letter words that are anagrams (rearrangements of the same letters) of one another.

1. Use _____ baseball bat if you want to get more _____.
2. Male cats are called _____ by _____ people.
3. The man _____ his _____ hat on the bus.
4. The old man related his _____ until _____ in the evening.
5. An _____ of land was the prize promised to the winner of the _____.
6. My finger is still _____ where I pricked it on the thorn of a _____.
7. It rained _____ and dogs on the _____ during the last two _____ of the play when it was performed in the park.
8. It was a _____ to clean the pots and _____ while the kids were taking their _____.

Cube Fold

Which of the twelve figures below would *not* form a perfect cube if it were folded along the dotted lines?

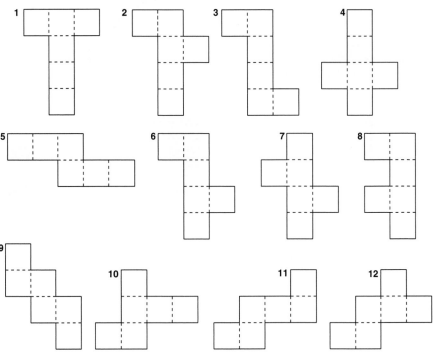

Answers on page 90.

Sign of the Times

Fill each square of the grid with a number between 1 and 9 so that the product of the digits in each row or column is equal to the number that appears at the end of that row (or bottom of that column.) Important: the number 1 can only be used once in any row or column; other numbers can be repeated.

Hint: Some of the squares contain 5s or 7s. Identify these first.

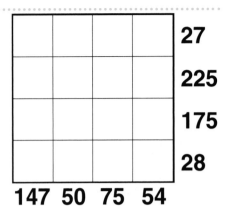

27
225
175
28

147 50 75 54

Spiral: Classic Movies

Spirals offer a novel twist on the crossword idea. Instead of words crossing, they overlap. The last letters of one word form the first letters of the next word. Words bend around corners as necessary—always heading inward toward the center of the spiral.

1. Greta _____
2. Humphrey _____
3. Actor, musician, or painter
4. _____ Laurel
5. "The Blue _____" (Marlene Dietrich movie)
6. _____ Burstyn
7. Bring enjoyment to audiences
8. Cowboy's traditional foe
9. _____ Bancroft
10. Patricia _____
11. Alan _____
12. _____ O. Selznick
13. _____ Lupino
14. Blythe _____
15. _____ Borgnine
16. _____ Parsons
17. Jack _____
18. Yves _____
19. _____ Warhol
20. _____ Cannon
21. _____ Lansbury
22. _____ Turner
23. 1968 Luis Buñuel film
24. _____ Starr

Answers on page 90.

What's for Dinner?

There are 18 differences between the top and the bottom scene of this family dinner. Can you find all of them?

Answers on page 90.

On the Plus Side

Fill in the missing spaces with numbers between 1 and 9. The numbers in each row must add up to the sums in the right-hand column. The numbers in each column must add up to the sums on the bottom line. The numbers in each diagonal must add up to the sums in the upper and lower right corners.

							26
2	3		8		3	5	34
3		3	9	1		7	31
	2	7		3	6	8	39
9		2	6	7	3		42
1	3		9		2	1	22
3	5	4	7		8		34
2	4	9			2	4	34
28	**27**	**32**	**49**	**32**	**28**	**40**	**36**

Overload of Os

Inside this picture is an overload of things beginning with the letter "O." We count 11 things. How many can you find?

Answers on page 90.

The Perfect Cube? MEMORY RECALL COMPUTATION

Fill in this crossword with numbers instead of letters. Use the clues to determine which of the numbers 1 through 9 belongs in each square. No zeros are used.

Hint: The complete list of three-digit cubes is: 125, 216, 343, 512, 729.

ACROSS

1. A multiple of 41
4. A number with the pattern AABC whose digits add up to 13
5. Consecutive odd digits, ascending
6. The sum of the first three digits is equal to the last digit
7. A cube

DOWN

1. A palindrome
2. Consecutive digits out of order
3. A cube that's also a square
4. A cube that's also a palindrome
5. A cube

Have a Taste, Bud

PROBLEM SOLVING

LANGUAGE   MEMORY

An independent research company decided to recreate a famous "taste test" commercial between Cola A and Cola B. Students in an advertising class would be blindfolded, given sips of each, and asked to identify the soda. Since it meant a day off from school, one hundred students applied to be participants. In order to be selected, a student had to have tasted both Cola A and Cola B. Thirteen students admitted their moms wouldn't let them drink anything but juice. Sixty-five of the students had tasted Cola A, and 78 had tasted Cola B. How many of the students had tasted both and would spend the rest of the day in the dark, sipping and burping?

Hint: Start by eliminating students who have tasted neither.

Answers on page 90.

Co-Starring

Two of these star fragments can be put together to form a perfect five-pointed star like the one here. Can you figure out which two pieces they are?

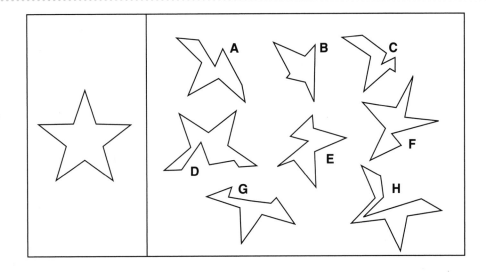

Twenty-Sided Triangle

Arrange the numbers 1 through 9—using each number once—in the squares below so that the numbers on each side add up to 20. There are several possible solutions.

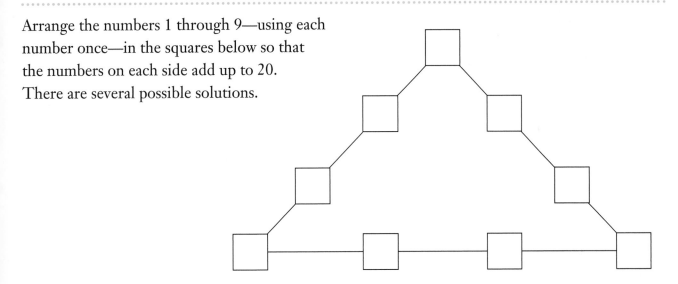

Next Letter?

What will be the next letter in this logical progression?

O, T, T, F, F, S, S, ____

Answers on page 90.

Girlfriends

Four women's names are hiding in this grid. Each name contains the letter "N" twice. The number of times each name appears is indicated in the circles in the four corners. The blanks next to the circles indicate the number of letters in each name. Can you fill in the four correct names? Names read left to right, right to left, top to bottom, bottom to top, and all four ways diagonally.

Word Ladder Fun

Change just one letter on each line to go from the top word to the bottom word. Do not change the order of the letters.

1. CALF
_____
_____
BULL

2. WORK
_____
_____
_____
REST

3. MOON
_____
_____
BEAM

4. TRAIN
_____
WRECK

5. HARD
_____
_____
SOFT

6. FOOL
_____
_____
WISE

Answers on page 90.

Square the Circle

All you have to do to solve this puzzle is move in a single, unbroken path from the circle in the upper left corner to the circle in the lower right. Your path must alternate between circles and squares, and you can only move vertically and horizontally (not diagonally). There are two ways to do it—can you find both?

⚙ Trivia on the Brain

Written sometime around 1,700 B.C., the Edwin Smith surgical papyrus contains the first recorded use of the word "brain."

Answers on page 91.

Car Chase

These people have had a great day shopping in the city! One problem: They can't find the parking garage to get their car. Can you help?

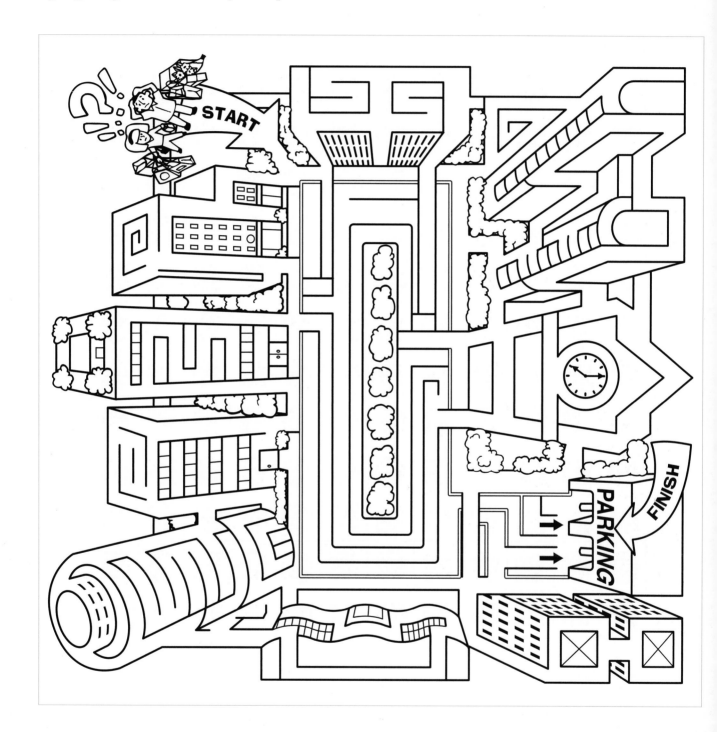

Answers on page 91.

Running the Numbers

Fill in this crossword with numbers instead of letters. Use the clues to determine which of the numbers 1 through 9 belongs in each square. No zeros are used.

Hint: The complete list of three-digit cubes is: 125, 216, 343, 512, 729.

ACROSS

1. A multiple of 14
3. Consecutive digits, ascending
6. Four consecutive even digits, in some order
7. A multiple of 2

DOWN

1. A cube
2. A palindrome
4. Consecutive digits, ascending
5. A square that's also a palindrome

Number Lock

Most of the numbers in the outer ring of this Number Lock equal the sum of two numbers in the inner ring. For example, 18 and 7 in the inner ring equal 25 in the outer ring. Three outer-ring numbers, however, do not fit this formula. Find the three oddball outer-ring numbers, then add them up to find a familiar solution.

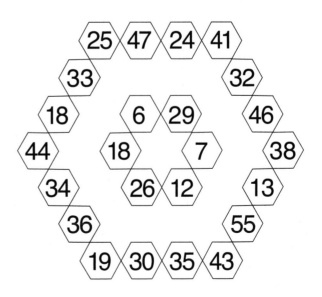

Answers on page 91.

Ten-Penny Challenge

Reverse the direction of this triangle—make it point downward—by moving only 3 of the 10 pennies.

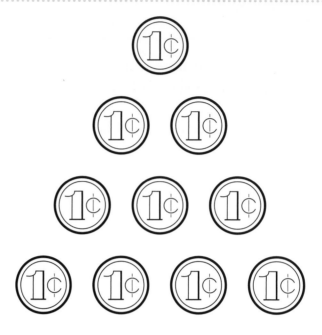

She's a Rich Girl

In a new twist on blind dates, a single woman who had just won $100,000 in the lottery offered to date to the first man who could guess her name. Since the woman wanted to date a smart guy, not just one who could say names really fast, she gave the following hint: Assign the letters of the alphabet to their numerical values. That means A = 1, B = 2, C = 3, up to Z = 26. Her first name has the letter values that, when multiplied together, equal exactly 100,000. While Louie the lounge lizard tried all of the names of women who had ever turned him down, Mike the macho mathematician got her name, the date, her heart, and a pre-nup. What was the woman's name?

Answers on page 91.

Name Game

Four names, two men's and two women's, can be found in this grid. The blanks next to each picture indicate how many letters are in each of their names. Reading from left to right, right to left, top to bottom, bottom to top, and all four ways diagonally, can you find the number of times each name appears? The grand total for all four names is 36.

We filled in one name to get you started.

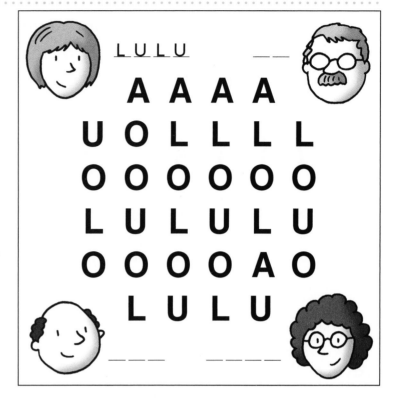

Number Fun

There are 14 numbers in the honeycomb below that are surrounded by different numbers (no numbers are repeated around them). Can you find them all?

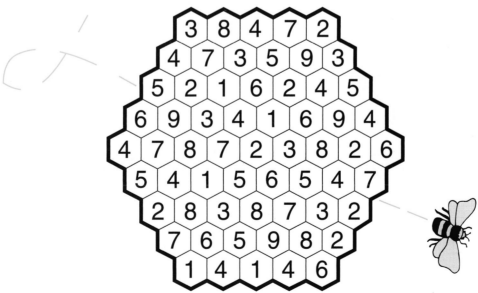

Answers on page 91.

INCREASE THE INTENSITY

In this section, the puzzles are more demanding, so get ready for some great mental exercise! To intensify the challenge, we've added cryptograms, word paths, number mazes, and visual memory exercises.

Word Paths

SPATIAL VISUALIZATION   **LANGUAGE**

Each of these word paths contains a familiar saying. To figure out the saying, read freely from letter to letter. Some letters will be used more than once. You can also move both forward and backward along the straight lines. The blanks indicate the number of letters in each word of the saying.

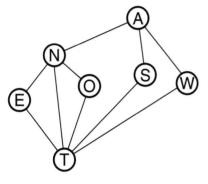

1. _ _ _ _ _   _ _ _ ,

    _ _ _ _   _ _ _

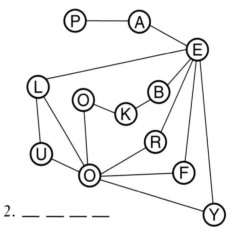

2. _ _ _ _

    _ _ _ _ _ _   _ _ _

    _ _ _ _

3. _ _ _ _ _ _ _ _

    _ _ _ _   _ _ _

    _ _ _ _ _

4. _   _ _ _ _ _ _ _

    _ _   _ _ _ _

    _ _ _ _ _   _ _ _ _

Answers on page 91.

An Actor's Bio

Cryptograms are messages in substitution code. Break the code to read the message. THE SMART CAT might become FVO QWGDF JGF if F is substituted for T, V for H, O for E, and so on. The code is different for each cryptogram.

Hint: Look for repeated letters. E, T, A, O, N, R, and I are the most often used letters. A single letter is usually A or I; OF, IS, and IT are common 2-letter words; THE and AND are common 3-letter groups.

LA   ZRY   MDWU-VR-MDWU   REWDXE   QRX   *WDBVDTYE*

WRIXDFARIE   DYP   *MRCE*   *VRZY.*   LA   DSER   EVDXXAP

TY   *QDVLAX*   *RQ*   *VLA*   *MXTPA.*   ZLR   TE   LA?

EBAYWAX   VXDWC

Number-Crossed

Fill in this crossword with numbers instead of letters. Use the clues to determine which of the numbers 1 through 9 belongs in each square. No zeros are used.

ACROSS
1. The two outside digits add up to the middle digit
4. A number with the pattern AABCC
6. A square
7. A multiple of 19
8. The sum of the first two digits is equal to the sum of the last three digits
10. A square

DOWN
1. Consecutive digits, ascending
2. A multiple of 13
3. Consecutive digits, descending
4. A cube
5. A square palindrome
9. A multiple of 17

Answers on page 91.

Sketchbook 1

Ambrose Anderson's granddaughter loved to draw. When she came home, she'd draw everything she could remember seeing that day. The top picture is one page from her sketchbook. Later on, she erased three of the drawings and replaced them with three new drawings. Study the top picture carefully, then turn the page upside-down to check out her revised sketchbook page. Without looking back at the top picture, can you circle the three drawings that are different?

What Month's Next?   PROBLEM SOLVING   ANALYSIS

What month comes next in this sequence?

April, August, December, February, ____

Answers on page 91.

Inward/Outward Bound

MEMORY **RECALL**

This puzzle requires an ability to think in circles. Guess the word that fits each clue, and place the letters in the numbered spaces which correspond to the number of letters in your answer. Work in both an outward and inward direction.

OUTWARD

1–4. Pale red

5–13. Ruckus

14–17. Nautical call

18–21. Tropical tree

22–26. Citrus fruit

27–31. Rub out

32–40. Passing

41–46. Disgust

47–52. Diamond or graphite

53–57. Apportion

58–62. Well known

63–68. Although

69–71. Macadamia, e.g.

72–74. And not

75–80. Weasel-like animal

INWARD

80–76. _____ Haute, Indiana

75–71. Façade

70–66. Loosen laces

65–61. Cutting part

60–56. The Lone Ranger's sidekick

55–51. Grassy plain (Spanish)

50–46. Support (oneself)

45–40. Servant's uniform

39–37. Rodent

36–33. Verne's captain

32–29. High plateau

28–25. Casino city

24–20. Fight

19–16. Knockout, briefly

15–11. Capital of Vietnam

10–8. Male cat

7–4. Ridicule

3–1. ___ it in the bud

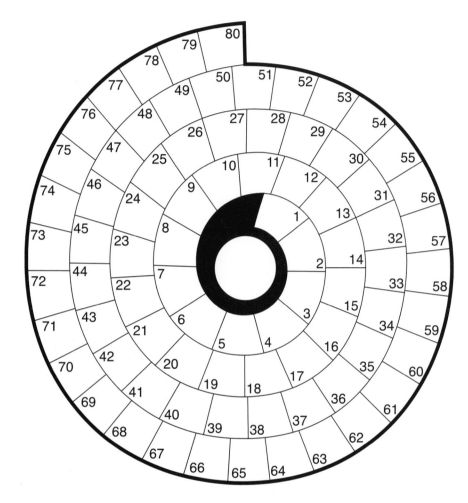

Answers on page 92.

Jigsaw

Rearrange these four jigsaw pieces into a square. If done properly, a capital letter will appear in the middle. Can you rearrange them and visualize the result using only your mind's eye?

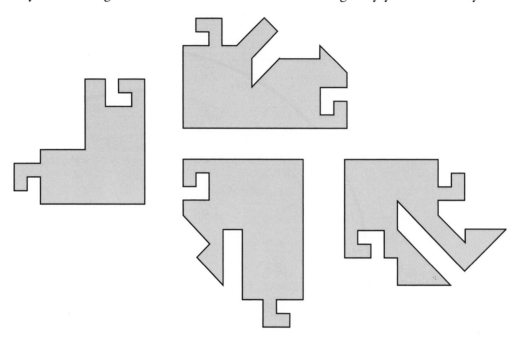

Can't Buy Me Lunch

Four friends met for lunch. When the check came, Cass, who had steak and potatoes, insisted that it could be fairly split into four equal parts. John, Denny, and Michelle, who ate three small but pricey salads, felt cheated. The check totaled 84 dollars, so Cass told each friend to put exactly four bills in front of them. Together, the 16 bills consisted of 4 ones, 8 fives, and 4 ten dollar bills. John had the least amount of money but had just one dollar less than Michelle. Cass had no ones but had the most money. Denny and Michelle were the only ones who had at least one of each bill. Each friend's four bills paid for their portion of the lunch. How much money did each person have?

Answers on page 92.

A Four-midable Maze

The object of this puzzle is to form a path from the "4" diamond on the left to the "4" diamond on the right. Move only through diamonds containing multiples of four. And move only through diamonds connected by a line.

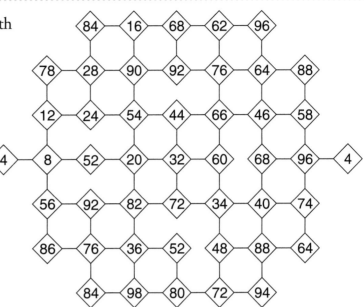

Hexagonal Shift Maze

Answers on page 92.

A Place in the United States

Cryptograms are messages in substitution code. Break the code to read the message. THE SMART CAT might become FVO QWGDF JGF if F is substituted for T, V for H, O for E, and so on. The code is different for each cryptogram.

Hint: Look for repeated letters. E, T, A, O, N, R, and I are the most often used letters. A single letter is usually A or I; OF, IS, and IT are common 2-letter words; THE and AND are common 3-letter groups.

VLXZ   VNT   MXVD   LJZ   VLB   AJVBFJD   JQML   JKU

VLB   EXZZNPQX   RNVJKXMJG   AJQUBK.   FLJV   XZ   XV?

ZV.   GNPXZ

Five-Letter Anagrams

Fill in the blanks in each sentence below with five-letter words that are anagrams (rearrangements of the same letters) of one another.

1. We _____ our car to _____, Delaware.

2. The guide took great _____ to point out that the capital of _____ is still Madrid.

3. She spilled ink, which left a permanent _____ on her new _____ dress.

4. The judge took a shortcut on the _____ through the woods to make it to the courtroom in time for the _____ .

5. _____ bread should at _____ be cheaper than fresh bread.

6. It is impolite to _____ at someone whose face is covered with _____ .

Answers on page 92.

Diagonal Thinking

Can you find a single, unbroken path from the circle in the upper left corner to the circle in the lower right? If you move horizontally or vertically, you must move only to the same shape (for example, from a square to a square). You must change shapes when you move diagonally. There's only one way to do it.

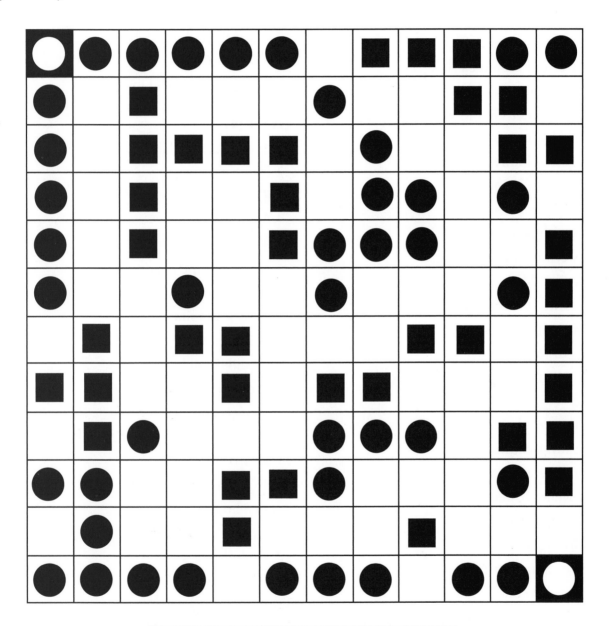

⚙⚙ **Trivia on the Brain**
After age 30, the brain shrinks a quarter of a percent in mass each year.

Answers on page 92.

Things Are Heating Up

ACROSS

1. Pottery class gunk
4. Drain the energy from
7. Actresses Evans and Hamilton
13. Opp. of WSW
14. President's time in office
16. Tiny critter seen on a slide
17. U.S. spy org.
18. Nobel winner Harold who discovered heavy hydrogen
19. Suggested indirectly
20. Little consolation
23. Summer in Paris
24. Clownish action
25. Western Hemisphere org.
26. Mo. after Mar.
28. One who stays calm during a tense situation
33. Game with Professor Plum
36. "___ to Joy"
37. Common way to fortify table salt
38. Fled
39. Chant sounds
40. Hockey great Bobby
41. Org. that sticks to its guns
42. Pay what is owed
44. Bullring cheer
45. Walrus relative
46. Not be a first-string player
49. "___ about time!"
50. ___ ___ glance
51. Partner of aahed
55. Unit of electrical resistance
57. Passionate
60. Realm

62. Prefix for logy or gram
63. First U.S. st.
64. ___ ___ ___ million
65. CNN offering
66. Pitcher's stat.
67. Turn the color of a beet
68. Queue after Q
69. Happy for glad: abbr.

DOWN

1. Holy city of Islam
2. Teamsters, e.g.
3. Did a poker task
4. Wall plaster
5. Early plane prefix
6. Casts a shape in advance
7. Cowardly Lion portrayer Bert
8. One who mimics
9. "Smoking or ___?"
10. Decide conclusively
11. Help in a crime
12. Marquis de ___
15. "Get outta ___ ___!" ("Stop hassling me!")
21. Craps cubes
22. Big Ten sch.
27. Pea holder
29. Energy or enthusiasm
30. Ambulance wail
31. Poet Pound
32. Actual
33. Gullet
34. Actress Turner
35. Like some beards or Christmas trees
39. Do better than
40. Shrub also known as a rose bay

43. Paramedic: abbr.
44. Get
45. Loafer, e.g.
47. Dine
48. Kelly to Regis
52. Lord of the underworld
53. Each

54. Raspy singer Bob
55. Smell
56. Sharpen, as a knife
58. Put ___ ___ act (pretend)
59. Mountain drinks?
61. Help

Counting Up

PROBLEM SOLVING   ANALYSIS

What is the next number in this common progression? What do these numbers represent?

$$1, 5, 10, 25, \underline{\quad}$$

Answers on page 92.

Circles and Numbers

Look at the circles and numbers below.
Replace the question mark with the correct number.

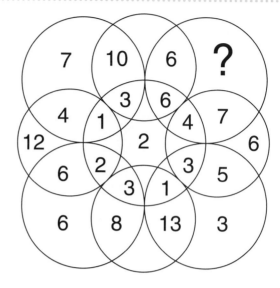

All in the Family

Three 3-letter family members can be found in this grid. MOM is the first. Additionally, each of their 3-letter first names can be found (one of which starts with the same letter as their position within the family). Every family member and each of their names appears the exact same number of times in the grid. Can you find them all reading left to right, right to left, top to bottom, bottom to top, and all four ways diagonally?

For extra credit, can you find the name of their hometown? It's five letters long, is a major U.S. city, and appears only once in the grid.

M O M: _ _ _

_ _ _ : _ _ _

_ _ _ : _ _ _

M	O	M	O	M
S	I	D	I	I
I	D	A	A	A
S	A	D	M	S
I	I	D	A	I
S	A	D	O	D

Their hometown: ____ ___ ___ ___

Trivia on the Brain

In 1504, Leonardo da Vinci produced wax casts of the ventricles of the human brain.

Answers on page 92.

Fifty State Highway

LANGUAGE

SPATIAL VISUALIZATION

Consider the grid below a super-highway that connects all 50 states. Can you connect them all?

4 Letters
IOWA
OHIO
UTAH

5 Letters
IDAHO
MAINE
TEXAS

6 Letters
ALASKA
HAWAII
KANSAS
NEVADA
OREGON

7 Letters
ALABAMA
ARIZONA
FLORIDA
GEORGIA
INDIANA
MONTANA
NEW YORK
VERMONT
WYOMING

8 Letters
ARKANSAS
COLORADO
DELAWARE
ILLINOIS
KENTUCKY
MARYLAND
MICHIGAN
MISSOURI
NEBRASKA
OKLAHOMA
VIRGINIA

9 Letters
LOUISIANA
MINNESOTA
NEW JERSEY
NEW MEXICO
TENNESSEE
WISCONSIN

10 Letters
CALIFORNIA
WASHINGTON

11 Letters
CONNECTICUT
MISSISSIPPI
NORTH DAKOTA
RHODE ISLAND
SOUTH DAKOTA

12 Letters
NEW HAMPSHIRE
PENNSYLVANIA
WEST VIRGINIA

13 Letters
MASSACHUSETTS
NORTH CAROLINA
SOUTH CAROLINA

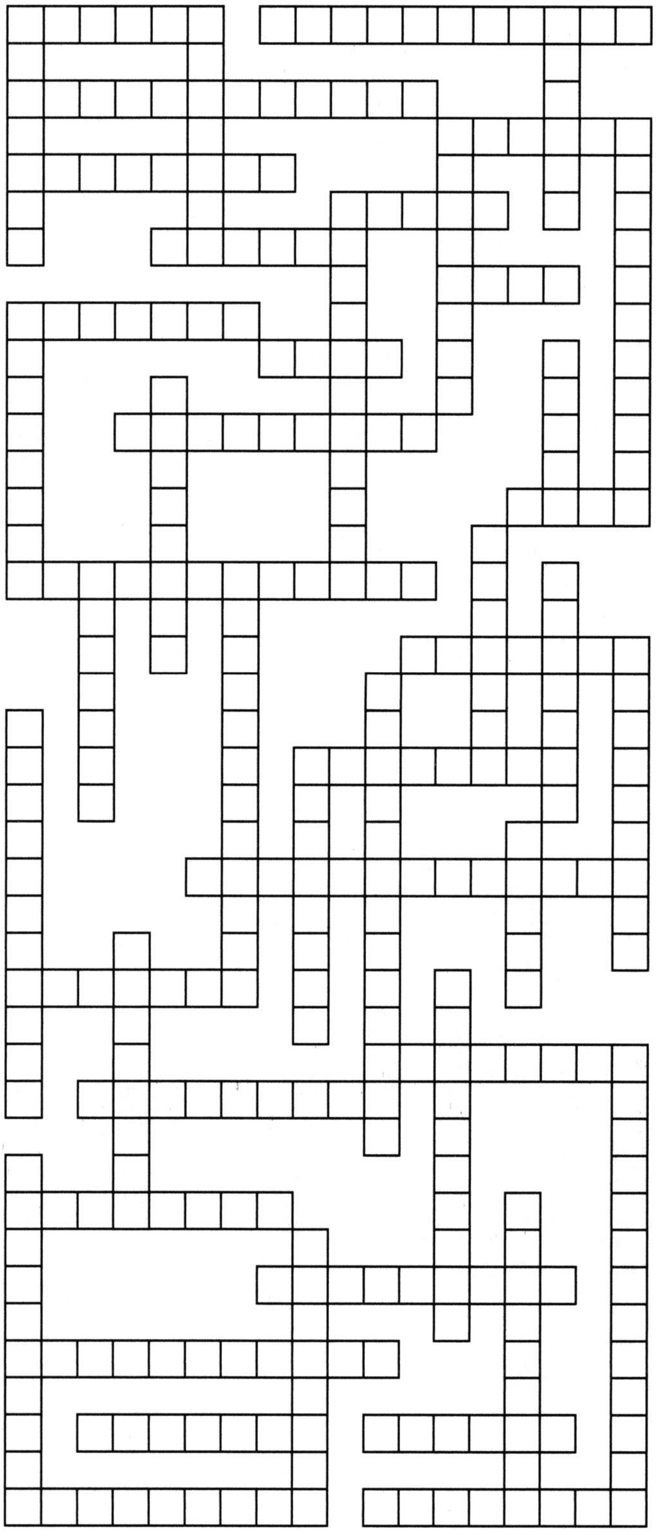

Answers on page 93.

A Lark in the Park

There are at least 14 differences between the top and bottom park scenes. Can you spot all of them?

Answers on page 93.

Cryptoquotes

PROBLEM SOLVING   LANGUAGE

Cryptograms are messages in substitution code. Break the code to read the message. THE SMART CAT might become FVO QWGDF JGF if F is substituted for T, V for H, O for E, and so on. The code is different for each cryptogram.

Hint: Look for repeated letters. E, T, A, O, N, R, and I are the most often used letters. A single letter is usually A or I; OF, IS, and IT are common 2-letter words; THE and AND are common 3-letter groups.

1. "WRLB,   OZ   XGRW   BX   XHFDRAYRD,   OD   SXB   WRLB

LHB   CS   OSYRDBERSB."

—ZFCSPAOS   W.   FXXDRYRAB

2. "UOB   LQ   OACOGPYD   QY   BY   URPO   BVGB   FVOA   FO

JYWO   BY   CRO   OPOA   BVO   LACODBGIOD   FRUU   XO

QYDDH."

—WGDI   BFGRA

Now's the Times

PROBLEM SOLVING   COMPUTATION

Fill each square of the grid with a number between 2 and 9 so that the product of the digits in each row or column is equal to the number that appears to the right of that row (or bottom of that column.) Important: This puzzle does not contain the number 1.

Hint: Factor each product into its component prime numbers. For example, 432 is 2×2×2×2×3×3×3.

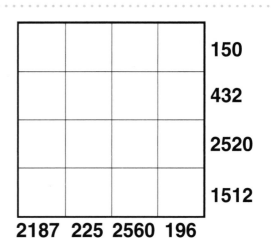

150

432

2520

1512

2187 225 2560 196

Answers on page 93.

Jigstars

These 12 jigsaw pieces can be put together to form six perfect six-pointed stars like the one pictured below. Using just your eyes, match up the correct pieces.

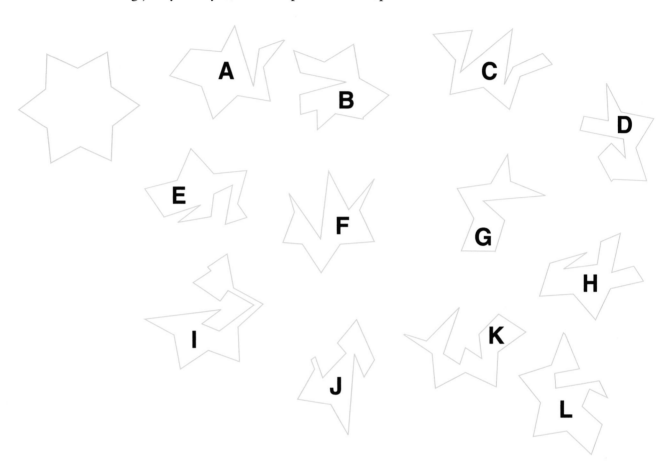

Ring of Numbers

Arrange the numbers 1 through 11 in the circles below, using each number once, so that any three numbers on a straight line add up to 18.

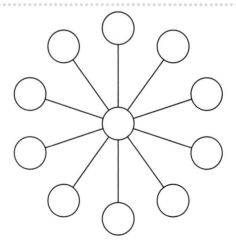

Answers on page 93.

Ovoids Maze

Digitally Mastered

MEMORY   RECALL   COMPUTATION

Fill in this crossword with numbers instead of letters. Use the clues to determine which of the numbers 1 through 9 belongs in each square. No zeros are used.

ACROSS

1. Three different even digits such that the first plus the second equals the third
4. Consecutive digits, ascending
6. Four consecutive digits, in some order
7. Its third digit is the sum of its first two digits

DOWN

1. Its first digit is the sum of its last two digits
2. A palindrome
3. The sum of its first two digits is equal to the two-digit number formed by its last two digits
5. A square

Answers on page 93.

We've saved the hardest puzzles for last! In this section, you'll find some new puzzles, including double crostics and mirror-image drawings.

Sum Puzzle   PROBLEM SOLVING   COMPUTATION

Using any of the numbers 1 through 9 as many times as you need to, fill in the blank squares so that each line, both vertically and horizontally, totals 30. There is only one way to do it.

2		4	5	7		3	2
	4	1	6			1	9
4			1		8	2	4
1	5			5			2
	6	1	3		4	2	6
7	3	4		2	5	1	
	1	6	7	1			2
1		2		3	2	5	

A Honey of a Puzzle   MEMORY   RECALL

Answer each definition with a six-letter word. Write the words clockwise around the numerals in the grid. Words overlap each other and may start in any of the spaces around the numerals. To assist you, we've placed some of the letters.

1. _____ the Pooh
2. Flowers from Holland
3. Struck lightly
4. Successful contestant
5. Escaped notice
6. More rosy
7. Two _____ don't make a right
8. Ukrainian port
9. Hot spring

Answers on page 93.

Mirror, Mirror

There's no trick here, only a challenge: Draw each of these familiar objects, then draw the mirror image of the same object. You may find it harder than you think!

Animal Riddles

Cryptograms are messages in substitution code. Break the code to read the message. THE SMART CAT might become FVO QWGDF JGF if F is substituted for T, V for H, O for E, and so on. The same code is used for each of these riddles.

1. IOGN'V   MEGTR   GJB   IOUNW   GJB   "PWB"   GEE   QFWP?

G   LWMPG   IWGPUJY   EUHVNUTR.

2. IOK   BUB   NOW   HQEUTW   GPPWVN   NOW   MUPB?

MWTGSVW   UN   IGV   G   PQMUJ.

By the Numbers

Fill in this crossword with numbers instead of letters. Use the clues to determine which of the numbers 1 through 9 belongs in each square. No zeros are used.

ACROSS

1. 17 less than 6-Across
3. 23 times 1-Down
5. Consecutive odd digits, ascending
6. A multiple of 23

DOWN

1. A prime number
2. A palindrome
3. Three consecutive digits, in some order
4. A perfect square

Answers on page 94.

Stack the Deck

This puzzle is actually two puzzles in one. For the first puzzle, find a single, unbroken path from the outlined spade in the upper left corner to the outlined club in the lower right corner. You can only move diagonally, and you must alternate between spades and clubs as you move. For the second puzzle, start at the outlined heart in the upper right corner and alternate between hearts and diamonds to find an unbroken path to the outlined diamond in the lower left corner.

Answers on page 94.

Double Crossed

To solve this double crostic, first answer as many of the clues as you can and write the answer to each in the corresponding blanks. The number under each blank indicates the square in the grid (containing the same number) where the answer letter belongs to complete a quotation. The small letters in the grid squares indicate what clue each answer letter is from to help guide you between the grid and the clues. Work back and forth between the grid and the clues until you complete the quotation.

1J	2A	3S		4R	5B	6D	7I		8M	9S	10F	11N		12B		13O	14P	15S	16G
17C	18R		19K	20Q	21A	22R	23G	24F		25K	26E	27P		28T	29F	30O		31Q	32B	33U
	34L	35I	36S	37R	38J	39E	40C		41S	42O		43S	44D	45K		46E	47L	48R	49H	50J
	51C	52S		53G	54S		55T	56J	57D	58N	59H	60P		61K	62N	63D		64H	65T
66G	67C	68Q	69M	70B	71D	72I		73N	74P		75K	76O	77C	78L	79T		80N	81E	
82C	83M	84I	85R	86Q	87O		88N	89O	90B	91H	92K	93C	94A	95U		96O	97Q	98F	
99I	100U	101K	102E	103J	104N		105I	106M	107K	108G	109H	110G	111Q	112T	113F	114B	115L		
	116K	117T	118M	119H		120P	121A	122O	123H	124C		125U	126F		127C		128R	129Q	130E	131B

A. Lepidopter
21 121 94 2

B. Memorial inscription
131 90 12 114 5 70 32

C. For lack of his love Echo died
17 127 93 67 51 124 40 77 82

D. Map
6 44 57 63 71

E. Treat with obsequious deference
130 26 39 81 102 46

F. Without difficulty
98 10 126 113 29 24

G. Caught
53 66 108 110 16 23

H. Spoiler
64 109 123 91 49 59 119

I. Tax
72 84 105 35 99 7

J. Famous
103 38 1 56 50

K. Church collection
107 61 25 45 101 116 92 19 75

L. Optimistic
78 47 34 115

M. Incensed
83 106 118 8 69

N. Throwing
11 62 88 58 80 73 104

Answers on page 94.

O. Fresh; vigorous

P. Long-limbed and slender

Q. Moral

R. Propose to give

S. Missed the mark

T. Without due consideration

U. Bonds

87	76	122	96	13	42	89	30
27	14	60	74	120
20	31	97	111	68	129	86
85	37	18	4	128	22	48
41	15	3	36	52	9	54	43
55	28	79	117	112	65
100	125	33	95

Chip off the Old Block

SPATIAL VISUALIZATION　　**PERCEPTION**

Is A, B, C, D, or E the missing piece from the broken cube? Try to solve this with your eyes only.

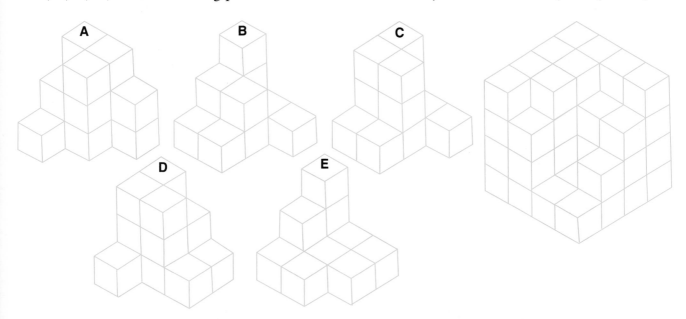

The Missing Numbers

PROBLEM SOLVING　　**ANALYSIS**

Each of these series of numbers follows a logical progression. What are the missing numbers?

A. 2, 5, ___, 11, 14

B. 10, 5, 12, ___, 14, ___, 16, 8

C. 2, 4, 8, ___, 32

D. 3, 5, 6, 8, 9, 11, ___

E. 28, 23, 19, 16, ___, 13

Answers on page 94.

Sketchbook 2

Ambrose Anderson's granddaughter is at it again—sketching everything she sees in her sketchbook. The top picture is a page from her sketchbook. But later on, she erased four of the drawings and replaced them with four new drawings. Study the top picture carefully, then turn the page upside-down to check out her revised sketchbook page. Without looking back at the top picture, can you circle the four drawings that are different?

Trivia on the Brain
Approximately 20 percent of the oxygenated blood flowing from the heart is pumped to the brain.

Answers on page 94.

Six-Letter Anagrams

Fill in the blanks in each sentence below with six-letter words that are anagrams (rearrangements of the same letters) of one another.

1. The athlete who _____ too hard without a break may _____ some of her muscles.

2. Those who _____ to greatness are often merely after the _____ and adulation of their peers.

3. It is a _____ feeling to know that a vigilant lifeguard will _____ you if you get into trouble while swimming.

4. When the sightseeing group _____ the south of France they came to a road under construction and had to _____ from their route.

5. My _____ and I could never _____ building a snowman in the winter.

6. I loathe close work so my _____ for sewing begins as soon as I _____ the needle.

State Capitals

Cryptograms are messages in substitution code. Break the code to read the message. For example, THE SMART CAT might become FVO QWGDF JGF if F is substituted for T, V for H, O for E, and so on. Each of the state capitals below uses the same code.

1. AYPARYRXIZAO, AY

2. QWYCRW, RG

3. LIYIZWZW, LA

4. ORNDRBCYJI, NR

5. RZHRYV, YV

6. NRDOIY NAJV, YF

7. QRNGOIY, BO

8. RWOJAY, JE

9. PIFCD, PC

10. JRZZRLROOCC, TZ

Answers on page 94.

ACROSS

1. Torch's crime
6. Works with a shuttle
10. D'Urbervilles lass
14. Plods along
19. French underground
20. "___ ___ long story"
21. Two-toned cookie
22. Get a bead on
23. Dog biters
24. Sewing connection
25. Jethro Bodine portrayer Max
26. Mirror sighting
27. "No thanks necessary"
29. "Something's not right here"
31. Stunning success
32. Abhor
34. Owl's cry
35. Without exception
39. Porgy's lady
40. "Dunno"
45. Fruit coloring agent
46. Gospel after Matthew
47. Stop nursing
48. Good earth
49. Over your head
50. Sampras of tennis
51. Poets with heroic themes
52. Seep slowly
53. Florida's Miami-___ County
54. Merit badge locale
55. Future tulips
56. Disk-shaped flower
57. 1977 sci-fi classic
59. Rock groups
60. Like formal attire
61. Letter enc.
62. "Outta sight!"
63. Diva highlight
64. Family cars

67. Cats' nine, proverbially
68. Golf course hazard
72. One way to order ham
73. Stared open-mouthed
74. Matador's opponent
75. Hydrant attachment
76. Weapon in some cafeteria fights
77. The whole shebang
78. Sound of amazement
79. Zoologists' study
80. "___ ___ want for Christmas …"
81. Sarcastic response
82. Tom, Dick, and Harry, e.g.
83. Military commando
84. Something many stores collect
86. Horse course
87. Hostile takeover artists
88. Attila, for one
89. "King Kong" star Fay
90. Actress Deborah
91. Working energetically
96. Any Tom, Dick, or Harry
102. Wedding seater
103. Holiday song
104. Russo of "Ransom"
105. Saint Teresa's home
106. Care for
107. Swiss mounts
108. One-named Irish singer
109. Track athlete
110. Get in shape
111. Eyelid ailment
112. Slightly
113. "Crocodile Rock" rocker John

DOWN

1. Switch on a radio
2. Swear by, with "on"
3. Ladder part
4. Out loud

5. Rocket's forward section
6. Thin paper
7. Consumed heartily
8. Former Russian ruler
9. "That goes for me too"
10. Way of being thrilled or torn
11. Wipe away
12. Come across as
13. Poor losers
14. Crew member
15. Type of bean
16. WWII General Bradley
17. Infatuated
18. Editor's notation
28. Top drawer
30. Bank offerings
33. Put the question to
35. Abacus counters
36. Chance to get a hit
37. Title role for Valerie Harper
38. Persevere
39. Rubber ducky's milieu
40. Some Yugoslavs
41. Within reach
42. Heckling sounds
43. Labyrinths
44. Manicurist's aid
46. Hodgepodge
47. Emerson's middle name
50. Remove the peel of
51. Short hits, in baseball
54. Mouth off to
55. Bleated
56. Lacking moisture
58. Taper off
59. Slanted surface
60. 1962 James Bond film
62. Try to bite
63. Golden agers' org.
64. Couch potatoes' perches

65. Name on a bomber
66. Amusing
67. Glove material
68. Run-of-the-mill
69. Cheek coloring
70. Emmy winner Ed
71. Bosc and anjou
73. Just lose it
74. What a dog may chase
77. Shakespeare's "___ Andronicus"

78. Uncertain subject
79. Legitimate target
82. Dam agcy.
83. ___ avis
85. Actress Stone
86. End of a threat
87. Take a second look at
89. Full of tears
90. Its capital is Nairobi
91. Head and shoulders

92. Web surfer
93. Queens stadium
94. Abominable snowman
95. Make a run for it
97. Air outlet
98. Villainous
99. Leave at the altar
100. Breakfast spread
101. Pull down

Answers on page 94.

Grid Computing

Each letter represents a number from 1 through 9. Use the clues to help you put the numbers in their correct places on the grid.

$A \times H = B \times F$

$H + D = B$

$D + B = F$

$B + F = C$

$B + E = J$

A	B	C
D	E	F
G	H	J

Multiples of Six Number Maze

Find your way through the maze. Start with the hexagon containing a 6 on the left, and finish with the hexagon containing a 6 on the right. Move from hexagon to hexagon only if there is a line connecting them, and only pass through hexagons containing multiples of 6.

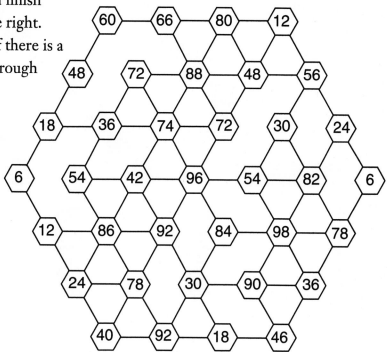

Answers on pages 94–95.

Equilateral Dismemberment

How many triangles are there in the larger figure?
How many are there in the smaller figure?
Are all of the triangles equilateral?

Similar Lines

Each of these groups contains a simile (___ as a ___) within it. Decipher the similes by moving from letter to letter. Some letters will be used more than once, and you may have to double back on some lines.

For example: (Answer: sly as a fox)

1.

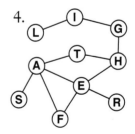

2.

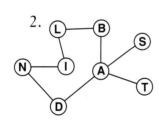

3.

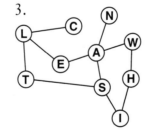

4.

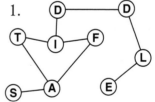

5.

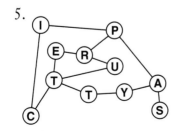

6.

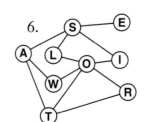

7.

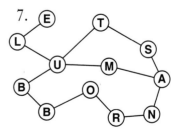

Answers on page 95.

Double the Fun

To solve this double crostic, first answer as many of the clues as you can, and write the answer to each in the corresponding blanks. The number under each blank indicates the square in the grid (containing the same number) where the answer letter belongs to complete a quotation. The small letters in the grid squares indicate what clue each answer letter is from to help guide you between the grid and the clues. Work back and forth between the grid and the clues until you complete the quotation.

1	2	3	4	5	6	7	8	9	10	11	12	13	14	15	16	17	18	19	20	21	22	23
					1H	2C	3F	4J	5L	6B		7I	8R	9A	10S	11H		12S	13P	14E	15F	
			16L	17B	18J	19S	20H	21K	22M		23G		24A	25F	26Q	27B	28M	29T		30R	31M	
	32F	33N	34O	35B	36A		37N	38B	39M	40P	41E	42H	43A	44D	45K	46J		47O	48G			
49S	50D	51A		52M	53K	54E	55B		56R	57F	58J	59I	60Q	61O		62F	63B	64M	65T	66S		
	67B	68E	69T		70H	71M	72J	73I	74A		75B	76F	77J	78R	79Q	80G						
81A	82I	83D	84O	85L	86E	87B	88Q		89E	90A		91S	92E	93I	94M	95O	96C	97P	98R		99T	100R
101K	102A	103T		104E	105P	106S	107K	108J		109H	110I		111C	112O	113B	114N	115P	116I	117M	118R		
	119L	120J	121R	122H	123G		124D	125A	126B		127T	128E	129R	130L	131B	132G	133Q	134C	135A	136F		
	137O		138K	139T	140N	141D	142R	143Q	144G		145L	146F	147K	148P	149M	150N	151T	152H	153G			
154F	155D	156C	157G	158E	159J	160R		161N	162B		163O	164F	165R	166M		167R	168B					
								169F	170K	171C	172S	173I	174L									

A. Murder
$\underline{\quad}_{9}\ \underline{\quad}_{24}\ \underline{\quad}_{36}\ \underline{\quad}_{43}\ \underline{\quad}_{51}\ \underline{\quad}_{74}\ \underline{\quad}_{81}\ \underline{\quad}_{90}\ \underline{\quad}_{102}\ \underline{\quad}_{125}\ \underline{\quad}_{135}$

B. "Arrangement in Grey and Black": 2 wds.
$\underline{\quad}_{6}\ \underline{\quad}_{63}\ \underline{\quad}_{27}\ \underline{\quad}_{55}\ \underline{\quad}_{67}\ \underline{\quad}_{75}\ \underline{\quad}_{87}\ \underline{\quad}_{113}\ \underline{\quad}_{126}\ \underline{\quad}_{131}\ \underline{\quad}_{162}\ \underline{\quad}_{168}\ \underline{\quad}_{17}\ \underline{\quad}_{35}\ \underline{\quad}_{38}$

C. Study of light
$\underline{\quad}_{2}\ \underline{\quad}_{111}\ \underline{\quad}_{134}\ \underline{\quad}_{96}\ \underline{\quad}_{156}\ \underline{\quad}_{171}$

D. Classic TV dog
$\underline{\quad}_{44}\ \underline{\quad}_{50}\ \underline{\quad}_{83}\ \underline{\quad}_{141}\ \underline{\quad}_{124}\ \underline{\quad}_{155}$

E. Chivalrous state
$\underline{\quad}_{104}\ \underline{\quad}_{14}\ \underline{\quad}_{41}\ \underline{\quad}_{54}\ \underline{\quad}_{68}\ \underline{\quad}_{86}\ \underline{\quad}_{92}\ \underline{\quad}_{89}\ \underline{\quad}_{128}\ \underline{\quad}_{158}$

F. The Big Apple, long ago: 2 wds.
$\underline{\quad}_{32}\ \underline{\quad}_{57}\ \underline{\quad}_{62}\ \underline{\quad}_{76}\ \underline{\quad}_{146}\ \underline{\quad}_{3}\ \underline{\quad}_{15}\ \underline{\quad}_{25}\ \underline{\quad}_{136}\ \underline{\quad}_{154}\ \underline{\quad}_{164}\ \underline{\quad}_{169}$

G. Fabled lost city
$\underline{\quad}_{23}\ \underline{\quad}_{48}\ \underline{\quad}_{123}\ \underline{\quad}_{132}\ \underline{\quad}_{144}\ \underline{\quad}_{153}\ \underline{\quad}_{157}\ \underline{\quad}_{80}$

H. Mann's "Magic"
$\underline{\quad}_{1}\ \underline{\quad}_{11}\ \underline{\quad}_{20}\ \underline{\quad}_{42}\ \underline{\quad}_{70}\ \underline{\quad}_{109}\ \underline{\quad}_{122}\ \underline{\quad}_{152}$

I. Foray
$\underline{\quad}_{7}\ \underline{\quad}_{73}\ \underline{\quad}_{59}\ \underline{\quad}_{93}\ \underline{\quad}_{110}\ \underline{\quad}_{116}\ \underline{\quad}_{173}\ \underline{\quad}_{82}$

J. Fictional female detective: 2 wds.
$\underline{\quad}_{108}\ \underline{\quad}_{58}\ \underline{\quad}_{120}\ \underline{\quad}_{4}\ \underline{\quad}_{46}\ \underline{\quad}_{77}\ \underline{\quad}_{18}\ \underline{\quad}_{159}\ \underline{\quad}_{72}$

K. Luminous insect
$\underline{\quad}_{21}\ \underline{\quad}_{45}\ \underline{\quad}_{53}\ \underline{\quad}_{101}\ \underline{\quad}_{107}\ \underline{\quad}_{170}\ \underline{\quad}_{138}\ \underline{\quad}_{147}$

Answers on page 95.

L. Gets the better of

M. Angling spot: 2 wds.

N. Main arteries

O. Sorcerer

P. Finale

Q. Mideast body of water: 2 wds.

R. Robert Sherwood play: 2 wds.

S. Spicy relish

T. Patronage

<u>5</u> <u>119</u> <u>130</u> <u>174</u> <u>145</u> <u>16</u> <u>85</u>

<u>31</u> <u>39</u> <u>117</u> <u>22</u> <u>64</u> <u>94</u> <u>149</u> <u>52</u> <u>71</u> <u>166</u> <u>28</u>

<u>33</u> <u>37</u> <u>150</u> <u>161</u> <u>114</u> <u>140</u>

<u>34</u> <u>112</u> <u>95</u> <u>47</u> <u>163</u> <u>84</u> <u>137</u> <u>61</u>

<u>13</u> <u>97</u> <u>115</u> <u>148</u> <u>105</u> <u>40</u>

<u>26</u> <u>60</u> <u>88</u> <u>133</u> <u>79</u> <u>143</u>

<u>142</u> <u>160</u> <u>167</u> <u>30</u> <u>100</u> <u>129</u> <u>8</u> <u>118</u> <u>165</u> <u>78</u> <u>98</u> <u>56</u> <u>121</u>

<u>172</u> <u>66</u> <u>19</u> <u>49</u> <u>91</u> <u>10</u> <u>106</u> <u>12</u>

<u>151</u> <u>139</u> <u>29</u> <u>127</u> <u>99</u> <u>65</u> <u>69</u> <u>103</u>

If You Come, They Will Build It

PROBLEM SOLVING   LANGUAGE   MEMORY

Donald and Ronald were two similar absent-minded builders with similar bad haircuts building similar apartment buildings in the same part of town. Upon completing two similar structures, each realized they had forgotten a very important part of the building. Jumping into their similar cars, they drove to the same building supply store. By chance, they met in the same aisle to pick up the same items. They noticed the items were priced as follows: 1 will cost $5. 5 will cost $5. 15 will cost $10. 1515 will cost $20. What items did both Donald and Ronald need?

Star Twenty-Six

PROBLEM SOLVING   COMPUTATION

Place the numbers 1 through 12 in the circles in the star below. Do it in such a way that any four numbers along a straight line add up to 26. Each number will be used only once.

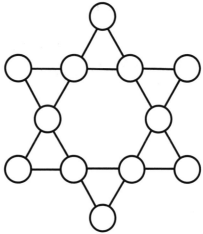

Answers on page 95.

On the Flip Side

There's no trick here, only a challenge: Draw each of these familiar objects, then draw the mirror image of the same object. You may find it harder than you think!

Cross-Country Trip

Start

Finish

Superfluity

Only 9 of these 12 boxes are usable in this puzzle. Your mission is to find the nine boxes that, when combined properly, form a capital letter. Try to do this with your eyes only.

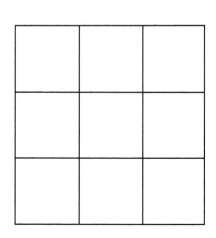

Answers on page 95.

ANSWERS

The House (page 6)

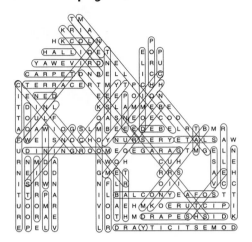

Anagrammed to Homonyms (page 7)

Real/reel; leek/leak; lane/lain; meat/meet; soar/sore

Seven Slices (page 7)

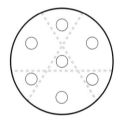

Patriotic Songs (pages 8–9)

JOLT	GAZE	ATEAM
AREA	ASIA	MILNE
REDLIGHTSPECIAL		
SOAKS		TEN
	NEARED	SATE
WHITECHRISTMAS		
AHAT	LEON	PEELS
BINGES		BALBOA
ARGON	ROLE	MANY
BLUESUEDESHOES		
ASPS	NEEDTO	
	ATA	BADGE
OLDGLORYSCOLORS		
REAPS	NOAH	ALAS
ANDSO	SUMO	NEMO

Don't Forget to Count the Donuts (page 10)

19

All Twenty-Six (page 11)

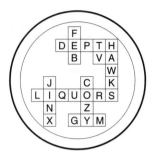

Assemblage of As (page 11)

Aardvark, abacus, airplane, air tank, alcove, ankles, apple, archer, arches, argyle socks, armor, arms, arrow, artichoke, astronaut, axe

Honeycomb (page 12)

Three-Letter Anagrams (page 12)

1. dad/add; 2. May/yam; 3. raw/war;
4. end/den; 5. ate/tea

It's Tricky! (page 14)

The items that don't belong to Jocko are the four linked rings (Jocko has three), the gloves with stars (Jocko's are white), and the cage with the gorilla (Jocko has a tiger).

The "T" Sound (page 15)

Leftover letters spell: T is for the tears she shed to save me

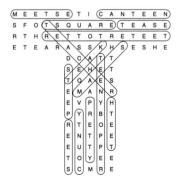

Lip Service (pages 16–17)

O	H	O	H	■	S	A	W	S	■	L	I	S	Z	T

Crossword solution grid:

```
O H O H ■ S A W S ■ L I S Z T
R E L O ■ H I Y O ■ A S H O E
B E D R O O M S L I P P E R S
S P E E D O ■ S E T S S A I L
■ ■ ■ B E T H ■ D E I ■ S S A
B A H ■ S P A R ■ M T G ■ ■ ■
A L A I ■ A R A B ■ U R G E S
B A R B E R S C L I P P E R S
E N E M Y ■ H E A D ■ S A L T
■ ■ ■ S E T ■ S N I T ■ R E S
I L E ■ G A P ■ D O R A ■ ■ ■
M E T A L L I C ■ C A L L M E
P A N C A K E F L I P P E R S
E D A M S ■ R O T E ■ H O E S
L A S E S ■ S S R S ■ A I D E
```

Rectangle Census (page 18)

13. Using the lettered diagram below, they are: ABH, BCD, DEF, FGH, B, D, F, H, J, E, DE, EF, EJ

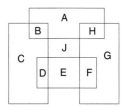

Hello, My Name Is Wrong (page 18)

Morey Money and Les Thyme

Maze: Soupy Sailfish (page 19)

Continuous Line Bet (page 20)

Sum-thing to Puzzle Over (page 20)

			15
①	2	③	6
4	⑤	6	15
7	8	⑨	24

12 15 18 15

Game On! (page 21)

M	E	G	A
G	A	M	E
A	G	E	M
E	M	A	G

Word Ladders (page 21)

1. Snap, slap, slat, slot, shot; 2. Milk, mill, mall, mail, pail; 3. Lake, lane, land, lend, lead, Mead; 4. Sail, soil, coil, coal, coat, boat; 5. Rose, ruse, rude, dude, duds, buds

Number Diamond (page 22)

The center circle must contain the number 5. The other 8 numbers can be arranged in several different combinations.

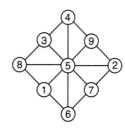

Bottom of the Dice (page 22)

There are 9 dots in all. On standard dice the numbers on opposite sides of a die always add up to 7.

Honeycomb Crossword (page 23)

More Word Ladders (page 23)

1. Foot, fool, foil, fail, fall, ball; 2. Snow, slow, slot, soot, foot, fort; 3. Side, tide, tile, tale, talk, walk; 4. Left, lift, lint, hint, hind, hand

Four-Letter Anagrams (page 24)

1. wand/dawn; 2. part/trap; 3. keep/peek; 4. spit/pits; 5. weak/wake; 6. Slow/owls; 7. mail/Lima; 8. ales/sale; 9. bowl/blow; 10. odor/door; 11. lime/mile; 12. care/race; 13. Abel/able; 14. Nile/line; 15. Alps/pals

Barbershop Duet (page 25)

1. Three men in the mirror; 2. Customer still has hair in mirror image; 3. Person hanging on coatrack; 4. Magazine is upside-down; 5. Sandwich and shoe shine on price list; 6. Everyone is bald; 7. Shampoo costs more than a haircut

Number Gridlock (page 25)

8	3	3	1
7	1	3	2
2	5	1	5
1	9	3	3

Jumble of Js (page 26)

Jacket, jack-in-the-box, jacks, jam, jar, jelly beans, jewelry, jingle bells (on hat), jump rope

It's Easier at the Dollar Store (page 26)

Sally could not buy items that cost $1, $3, $67, or $69.

Around the World in 20 Minutes (page 27)

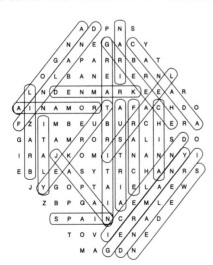

Crossing Caution (pages 28–29)

Word of Mouth (page 30)

T	O	H	U	M
H	U	M	T	O
M	T	O	H	U
O	H	U	M	T
U	M	T	O	H

What's Flipped in Vegas, Stays in Vegas (page 30)

The coin came up heads 12 times.

Match-Up Twins (page 31)

The matching pairs are: 1 and 8, 2 and 9, 3 and 6, 4 and 7, 5 and 10.

Add It Up (page 32)

						25
②	4	6	⑧	2	4	26
1	③	⑤	7	9	1	26
4	6	8	②	4	⑥	30
9	⑦	5	3	①	9	34
2	4	⑥	8	1	③	24
①	3	5	7	⑨	1	26
19	27	35	35	26	24	18

Age-Old Question (page 32)

My birthday is December 31st. The day I made the statement was January 1st. So, 2 days ago (December 30th) I was 18, and on December 31st I turned 19; I will be 20 on December 31st of this year, and next year on December 31st I will be 21.

Retro Rocket Maze (page 33)

Take a Number (page 34)

2	3	4		
5	2	5	2	
	3	6	6	3
		7	8	9

Name Search (page 34)

ROB wins. His name appears 13 times. BOB, even though it can be spelled forward and backward, appears only 12 times. The word ORB is hidden twice.

Circle Takes the Square (page 35)

Letters to Numbers (page 36)

8	1	6
3	5	7
4	9	2

Art for Art's Sake? (page 36)

Model facing wrong direction; model wearing different clothes in painting; picture on wall overlaps easel; turtle on painter's head; palette floating in midair; easel and model not on floor; chair missing in painting; model watching television; whistle around painter's neck

Can You Conjugate a Beatle? (page 37)

John

Number Challenge (page 37)

2	1		6	1
2	3	4	5	6
	7	7	5	
7	9	3	5	1
7	5		6	5

To the Letter (page 38)

A	B	C	D	E	F
3	5	1	2	4	7

Misleading Sequence (page 38)

12 + 6 = 18

Next Color? (page 38)

The next color is black, the color of the eight-ball in pool.

Diagonal Switch (page 39)

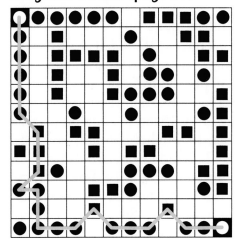

Awfully Nice (pages 40–41)

A	S	I	A	■	E	L	B	A	■	L	I	M	O	S
L	A	C	S	■	C	O	O	L	■	I	L	O	V	E
G	U	E	S	T	H	O	S	T	■	F	L	U	E	S
E	N	R	O	B	E	■	S	A	M	E	H	E	R	E
R	A	S	C	A	L	■	A	R	O	S	E	■	■	
■	■		R	O	T	■	S	T	P	A	U	L	S	
P	E	S	O	■	N	A	P	■	H	A	L	V	E	S
E	P	O	X	Y	■	P	E	T	■	N	T	E	S	T
R	E	D	Y	E	D	■	Z	A	P	■	H	A	T	S
T	E	A	M	S	U	P	■	G	A	G	■	■		
■	■		O	S	O	L	E	■	P	O	S	S	E	S
R	E	P	R	I	S	A	L	■	A	N	E	M	I	A
E	R	R	O	R	■	G	O	O	D	G	R	I	E	F
A	L	I	N	E	■	U	P	T	O	■	A	L	I	E
R	E	E	S	E	■	E	E	O	C	■	C	E	O	S

Anagrammatically Correct (page 42)

1. this/hits; 2. toms/most; 3. left/felt;
4. tale/late; 5. acre/race; 6. sore/rose;
7. cats/cast/acts; 8. snap/pans/naps

Cube Fold (page 42)

Figure 8

Sign of the Times (page 43)

3	1	3	3
1	5	5	9
7	5	5	1
7	2	1	2

Spiral: Classic Movies (page 43)

G	A	R	B	O	G	A
N	E	A	L	D	A	R
N	O	N	T	A	V	T
A	M	A	R	N	I	I
I	M	Z	I	D	D	S
D	E	A	N	Y	A	T
N	L	N	G	A	N	A
I	L	A	O	N	N	N
A	E	L	E	G	E	G
T	T	S	E	N	R	E
R	E	T	N	E	L	L

What's for Dinner? (page 44)

In the bottom picture: 1. Rounded chair back;
2. Girl has soldier toy; 3. Girl wearing black
skirt; 4. Bowl on plate in front of girl; 5. Sail-
boat flag points right; 6. Man wearing bowtie;
7. Man holding screwdriver; 8. Ham on platter;
9. Corn on table; 10. Pitcher half full; 11. Cake
on windowsill; 12. Window has two panes;
13. Square pattern on curtain; 14. Boy is eating
yams; 15. Boy is wearing sweater; 16. Woman
not wearing oven mitts; 17. Square tray cover;
18. Woman's apron is different

On the Plus Side (page 45)

							26
2	3	(6)	8	(7)	3	5	34
3	(4)	3	9	1	(4)	7	31
(8)	2	7	(5)	3	6	8	39
9	(6)	2	6	7	3	(9)	42
1	3	(1)	9	(5)	2	1	22
3	5	4	7	(1)	8	(6)	34
2	4	9	(5)	(8)	2	4	34
28	27	32	49	32	28	40	36

Overload of Os (page 45)

Obelisk, octagon, octopus, oil can, olives,
onion, ostrich, ottoman, outboard engine,
outlet, oven

The Perfect Cube? (page 46)

■		2	8	7
	1	1	9	2
1	3	5	7	9
2	3	1	6	■
5	1	2	■	■

Have a Taste, Bud (page 46)

56 students have tasted both Cola A and Cola B.

Co-Starring (page 47)

A and E are the correct pieces.

Twenty-Sided Triangle (page 47)

Two possible solutions are:

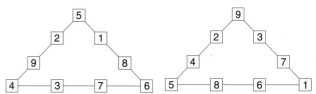

Next Letter? (page 47)

E as in eight. The other letters are the first
letters of the numbers one through seven.

Girlfriends (page 48)

NAN appears 24 times. ANN appears 18 times.
ANNA appears 6 times, and NANA appears
3 times.

Word Ladder Fun (page 48)

1. Calf, call, ball, bull; 2. Work, pork, port,
pert, pest, rest; 3. Moon, moan, mean, bean,
beam; 4. Train, trait, tract, track, wrack, wreck;
5. Hard, card, care, core, sore, sort, soft;
6. Fool, foot, loot, lost, list, lisp, wisp, wise

Square the Circle (page 49)

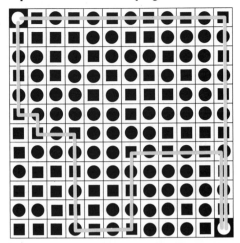

Car Chase (page 50)

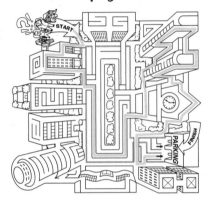

Running the Numbers (page 51)

5	6		
1	2	3	4
2	6	4	8
		5	4

Number Lock (page 51)

34 + 43 + 46 = 123

Ten-Penny Challenge (page 52)

Move pennies 1, 7, and 10 as shown to reverse the triangle.

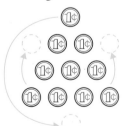

She's a Rich Girl (page 52)

Betty

Name Game (page 53)

LULU appears 4 times, LOLA 5 times, AL 11 times, and LOU 16 times.

Number Fun (page 53)

Word Paths (page 54)

1. Waste not, want not; 2. Look before you leap; 3. Practice what you preach; 4. A stitch in time saves nine

An Actor's Bio (page 55)

He won back-to-back Oscars for *Captains Courageous* and *Boys Town*. He also starred in *Father of the Bride*. Who is he?
Spencer Tracy

Number-Crossed (page 55)

	4	9	5	
5	5	1	4	4
1	6		3	8
2	7	3	2	4
	8	4	1	

Sketchbook 1 (page 56)

What Month's Next? (page 56)

The order is alphabetical, and the next month is January.

Inward/Outward Bound (page 57)

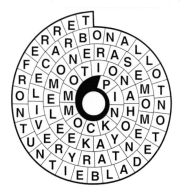

Jigsaw (page 58)

Can't Buy Me Lunch (page 58)

Denny had 1 one, 2 fives, and 1 ten for a total of $21. Michelle had 2 ones, 1 five, and 1 ten for a total of $17. John had 1 one, 3 fives, and no tens for a total of $16. Cass had no ones, 2 fives, and 2 tens for a total of $30.

A Four-midable Maze (page 59)

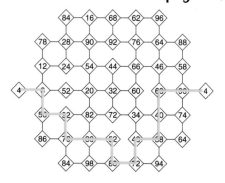

Hexagonal Shift Maze (page 59)

A Place in the United States (page 60)

This top city has the Gateway Arch and the Missouri Botanical Garden. What is it? St. Louis

Five-Letter Anagrams (page 60)

1. drove/Dover; 2. pains/Spain; 3. stain/satin; 4. trail/trial; 5. stale/least; 6. stare/tears

Diagonal Thinking (page 61)

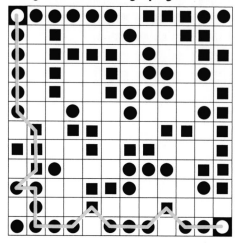

Things Are Heating Up (pages 62–63)

Counting Up (page 63)

These numbers represent the value of U.S. coins. The next number is 50.

Circles and Numbers (page 64)

Replace the question mark with a 2—the numbers in each circle total 25.

All in the Family (page 64)

MOM is MIA. DAD is SID. SIS is IDA. Each appears four times. Their hometown is MIAMI.

Fifty State Highway (page 65)

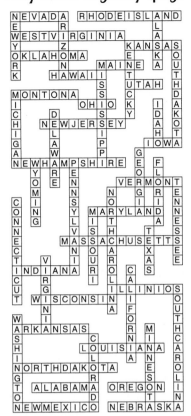

A Lark in the Park (page 66)

In the bottom picture: 1. Woman wearing heels; 2. Baby in shopping cart; 3. Blimp; 4. Child has balloon in left hand; 5. Statue holding broom; 6. Kite has no tail; 7. Skater wearing earmuffs; 8. Cat in tree; 9. Jogger has ponytail; 10. Jogger wearing black shorts; 11. Dog has no spots; 12. Round street lamp; 13. Boy on bench doesn't have legs crossed; 14. Man is reading "News"

Cryptoquotes (page 67)

1. "Debt, if owed to ourselves, is not debt but an investment."
—Franklin D. Roosevelt

2. "Let us endeavor so to live that when we come to die even the undertaker will be sorry."
—Mark Twain

Now's the Times (page 67)

3	5	5	2
9	3	8	2
9	5	8	7
9	3	8	7

Jigstars (page 68)

The pairs are: A and G, B and K, C and F, D and L, E and H, I and J.

Ring of Numbers (page 68)

The 6 must go in the center circle, and each set of opposite circles must add up to 12.

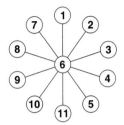

Ovoids Maze (page 69)

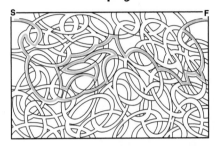

Digitally Mastered (page 69)

6	2	8	■
3	4	5	6
3	4	1	2
■	2	3	5

Sum Puzzle (page 70)

2	①	4	5	7	⑥	3	2
④	4	1	6	②	1	9	③
4	②	⑤	1	④	8	2	4
1	5	⑦	②	5	③	⑤	2
②	6	1	3	⑥	4	2	6
7	3	4	①	2	5	1	⑦
⑨	1	6	7	1	①	③	2
1	⑧	2	⑤	3	2	5	④

A Honey of a Puzzle (page 70)

Animal Riddles (page 72)

1. What's black and white and "red" all over?
A zebra wearing lipstick.
2. Why did the police arrest the bird?
Because it was a robin.

By the Numbers (page 72)

		2	9
5	2	2	1
3	5	7	9
4	6		

Stack the Deck (page 73)

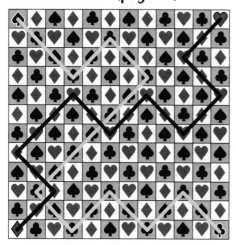

Double Crossed (pages 74–75)

"The fact that I have no remedy for all the sorrows of the world is no reason for my accepting yours. It simply supports the strong probability that yours is a fake."
—H. L. Mencken, *Minority Report*

A. Moth; B. Epitaph; C. Narcissus; D. Chart;
E. Kowtow; F. Easily; G. Nabbed; H. Marplot;
I. Impost; J. Noted; K. Offertory; L. Rosy;
M. Irate; N. Tossing; O. Youthful; P. Rangy;
Q. Ethical; R. Proffer; S. Overshot; T. Rashly;
U. Ties

Chip off the Old Block (page 75)

The correct piece is D.

The Missing Numbers (page 75)

A. 8; B. 6, 7; C. 16; D. 12; E. 14

Sketchbook 2 (page 76)

Six-Letter Anagrams (page 77)

1. trains/strain; 2. aspire/praise;
3. secure/rescue; 4. toured/detour;
5. sister/resist; 6. hatred/thread

State Capitals (page 77)

1. Indianapolis, IN; 2. Juneau, AK; 3. Honolulu, HI; 4. Sacramento, CA; 5. Albany, NY;
6. Carson City, NV; 7. Jackson, MS; 8. Austin, TX; 9. Dover, DE; 10. Tallahassee, FL

Celebrity Disputes (pages 78–79)

A	R	S	O	N		T	A	T	S		T	E	S	S		S	L	O	G	S
M	E	T	R	O		I	T	S	A		O	R	E	O		A	I	M	A	T
F	L	E	A	S		S	E	A	M		B	A	E	R		I	M	A	G	E
M	Y	P	L	E	A	S	U	R	E		I	S	M	E	L	L	A	R	A	T
				C	O	U	P		H	A	T	E		H	O	O				
B	A	R	N	O	N	E		B	E	S	S		S	E	A	R	C	H	M	E
E	T	H	E	N	E		M	A	R	K		W	E	A	N		L	O	A	M
A	B	O	V	E		P	E	T	E		B	A	R	D	S		O	O	Z	E
D	A	D	E		S	A	S	H		B	U	L	B	S		A	S	T	E	R
S	T	A	R	W	A	R	S		B	A	N	D	S		D	R	E	S	S	Y
		S	A	S	E		N	E	A	T	O		A	R	I	A				
S	E	D	A	N	S		L	I	V	E	S		S	A	N	D	T	R	A	P
O	N	R	Y	E		G	A	P	E	D		T	O	R	O		H	O	S	E
F	O	O	D		T	O	T	A	L		G	A	S	P		F	A	U	N	A
A	L	L	I		I	B	E	T		T	R	I	O		R	A	N	G	E	R
S	A	L	E	S	T	A	X		O	V	A	L		R	A	I	D	E	R	S
			H	U	N		W	R	A	Y		K	E	R	R					
B	U	S	Y	A	S	A	B	E	E		A	V	E	R	A	G	E	J	O	E
U	S	H	E	R		N	O	E	L		R	E	N	E		A	V	I	L	A
S	E	E	T	O		A	L	P	S		E	N	Y	A		M	I	L	E	R
T	R	A	I	N		S	T	Y	E		A	T	A	D		E	L	T	O	N

Grid Computing (page 80)

A 6	B 3	C 7
D 1	E 5	F 4
G 9	H 2	J 8

Multiples of Six Number Maze (page 80)

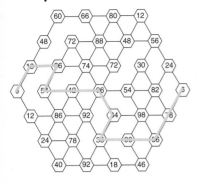

Star Twenty-Six (page 83)

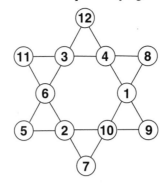

Equilateral Dismemberment (page 81)
Each figure contains 120 equilateral triangles.

Similar Lines (page 81)
1. Fit as a fiddle; 2. Blind as a bat; 3. Clean as a whistle; 4. Light as a feather; 5. Pretty as a picture; 6. Slow as a tortoise; 7. Stubborn as a mule

Double the Fun (pages 82–83)
"Moscow, Idaho . . . went through a series of names . . . . Originally it was Hog's Heaven . . . which the town's ladies insisted on changing. It was known as Paradise until its . . . postmaster, a Russian immigrant, decided to call it Moscow."
—Allan Wolk, *The Naming of America*

A. Assassinate; B. Whistler's Mother; C. Optics; D. Lassie; E. Knighthood; F. New Amsterdam; G. Atlantis; H. Mountain; I. Invasion; J. Nancy Drew; K. Glowworm; L. Outwits; M. Fishing hole; N. Aortas; O. Magician; P. Ending; Q. Red Sea; R. Idiot's Delight; S. Chowchow; T. Auspices

If You Come, They Will Build It (page 83)
Both needed address numbers for their buildings. Each digit costs $5, so 15 costs $10 and 1515 costs $20.

Cross-Country Trip (page 85)

Superfluity (page 85)
The superfluous letter parts are the second one from the left in the top row, the second one on the right in the middle row, and the one on the far left in the bottom row. The remaining nine letter parts form the capital letter "R" as shown below.

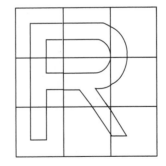

INDEX OF PUZZLES BY TYPE